TALLY'S CORNER

Legacies of Social Thought
Series Editor: Charles Lemert

TALLY'S CORNER

A Study of Negro Streetcorner Men

New Edition

ELLIOT LIEBOW

ROWMAN & LITTLEFIELD PUBLISHERS, INC.
Lanham • Boulder • New York • Toronto • Oxford

ROWMAN & LITTLEFIELD PUBLISHERS, INC.

Published in the United States of America
by Rowman & Littlefield Publishers, Inc.
A wholly owned subsidiary of the Rowman & Littlefield Publishing Group
4501 Forbes Boulevard, Suite 200, Lanham, Maryland 20706
www.rowmanlittlefield.com

P.O. Box 317, Oxford OX2 9RU, United Kingdom

British Library Cataloguing in Publication Information Available

Library of Congress Cataloging-in-Publication Data

Liebow, Elliot.
    Tally's corner : a study of Negro streetcorner men / Elliot Liebow.—
New ed.
        p.   cm.—(Legacies of social thought)
    ISBN 0-7425-2895-2 (cloth : alk. paper) — ISBN 0-7425-2896-0 (pbk. :
alk. paper)
    1. African American men—Washington (D.C.)—Social conditions—20th
century.   2. African Americans—Washington (D.C.)—Social
conditions—20th century.   3. African Americans—Social
conditions—1964–1975.   4. Urban poor—Washington (D.C.)—History—
20th century.   5. Washington (D.C.)—Social conditions—20th century.   I.
Title.   II. Series.
E185.93.D6L5   2003
305.896'0730753—dc21   2003008589

Printed in the United States of America

⊗ ™ The paper used in this publication meets the minimum requirements of
American National Standard for Information Sciences—Permanence of Paper for
Printed Library Materials, ANSI/NISO Z39.48-1992.

CONTENTS

FOREWORD TO THE 2003 EDITION

Tally's Corner and the Black Man of the City

CHARLES LEMERT

S ince it first appeared in 1967, Elliot Liebow's *Tally's Corner* has been read continuously by scholars, teachers, and students, among many others—by, that is, those concerned with the suffering of the urban poor. In the social and human sciences, only a handful of books have sold more than a million copies as this one has. A good many Americans (and not a few others around the world), including some without benefit of a college reading list, know what they know about the plight of the economically marginalized Black man in urban America through this one book. Some have heard the book's story even when they may never have heard (or have heard and forgotten) the names of the author or the book.

The influence of *Tally's Corner* on the thinking of some generations of policymakers, social activists, and coffee shop philosophers flows on the subterranean streams whereby public lessons drift without acknowledgment in the mist of sermons, newspaper essays, public speeches of all kinds, television talk shows, neighborhood grousings, and the myriad ways that public opinion is shaped. Whenever and wherever people come out of the dark to face the shadow of America's befuddled relation to the Black man of the city, *Tally's Corner* is somewhere in the penumbra of consciousness, serving as a lifeline against the currents of ill-informed racist blather about urban poverty.

Why? Why does so small a book have so large an importance? What accounts for the enduring value of a book of the urban long-ago before the global economy shattered the economic hopes of poor men in the American inner city? The book itself is plainly written—so plainly as to be deceptive. Some may think it, if not quaint, at least out of sociological fashion, if only for the key word in its subtitle, *A Study of Negro Streetcorner Men*. In those days the term "Negro" had not given up its place of racial pride to "Black" (very often with a capital *B* to reflect the capital *N* that W. E. B. Du Bois fought to insert upon public uses of "Negro"). Yet, readers of this 2003 Rowman & Littlefield edition will be surprised—and not just by the need to translate a few of the words and monetary figures or to imagine Tally's Corner reset amid the decline of employment prospects and the political economy of the drug trade that ravage the urban poor. What few translations may be required will be more than compensated by the abundant take from a story that reads so well and clarifies so sharply so many years after its first telling.

Tally's Corner continues to reward the reader in many ways and remains pertinent to an impertinent age. This book is, first, very good literature of a special kind—thus a relief from the drone of formal academic writing. Also among the gains from Elliott Liebow's literary gifts, *Tally's Corner* reads, even today, as sensible and compelling empirical social science, especially for the originality with which it avoids the clumsiness of many ethnographic studies. It is, thus, a book that rewards reading and learning not so much with pleasure as with the painful recognition that American race troubles remain so stubbornly at the center of social and economic life.

Any author would be delighted to have made even a single contribution. Few even dream of making so many. If we who have read and reread this book over many years owe Elliot Liebow our gratitude for making so many, we also owe his spirit a word of regret for not having expressed our debts during his lifetime. Re-reading and rethinking the importance of the book is an effort to fill the silence that outran the time.

Great literature usually invites the literary imagination into some local place. Very often those places are so powerfully conveyed that they are implanted in the consciousness. Among fictional places, one thinks of Homer's Ithaca, James Joyce's Dublin, William Faulkner's Yoknapatawpah County in Mississippi, and Ralph Ellison's Harlem. But how does the literary imagination work this marvel? How does an author compose a story upon a local place so as to cause it to grow mysteriously in the minds and hearts of readers who are unlikely ever to have visited the place— or, if they have, are unlikely to have seen it as the author has?

If by literary one means *fiction* or epic poetry, it would appear that the trick is turned by some hard-to-define, evocative connection between the imagination of the author and the feelings of readers. The first and deepest contact an author makes with her reader is at the level of feeling, as opposed to intellect, for it is feelings that have the power to unite readers one with the other into a community of an indefinite sort. The writer of fiction composes out of her private space a public imaginary into which many others can and do come. A fiction may in fact tell the truth very well, but its author bears no final responsibility to prove anything to anyone—only to evoke interestingly. The reader grants her safe passage even when he might know the place described well enough to judge the facts in the story. We read literary fiction not for the proven facts but for the feelings, the arousal of which may well lead to a fresh inspection of the facts of some general aspect of accessible reality.

If, however, by literary one means any of the forms of *nonfiction,* the mysteries must work somewhat, if not entirely, differently. Here one comes upon the distinctive responsibilities of literary work in the social sciences, of which none is more available to literary treatment than ethnographies like *Tally's Corner.* Unlike fiction, ethnography (which, after all, means "writing about a people") depends on the facts of the story, even when the reader is in no position to check them. When the realities are troubling, the author must tell the story as it is. Narratives that claim the legitimate cover of social science put their authors in a multifarious literary situation. You might say that social science is literature without the license. Social scientists are licensed differently—or, better put, what literary freedoms they may enjoy are bound by duty to their science. At the same time, the science in the writing is subject to public scrutiny and on occasion may be put at risk by events over which the author has no control.

One of the signs of Elliot Liebow's literary accomplishment is that he avoided the furor caused by a 1965 report on the very subject of his book—the Black man of the city. That report was, of course, Daniel Patrick Moynihan's *The Negro Family: A Case for National Action,* in which he naively assumed that the sugar of science would coat the bitter pill of what he called "the tangle of pathology"—of which the domestic failures of the Black man were the presenting symptom. Liebow's book was, if anything, more honest about the impoverishment of Black manhood in the cities, but he wrote with a grace that, while not comforting, was not provocative.[1] The idea is to evoke, not provoke. Liebow did this uncommonly well.

---

1. Liebow refers to the Moynihan report in the references, where it is listed under its official name as a report of the Office of Policy Planning and Research in the United States Department of Labor. Otherwise there is no mention of Moynihan's *The Negro Family: The Case for National Action.*

It might be assumed that Liebow found his way through the storm because he told the brutal truths in the words of Tally and the other men of the street corner. The equivalent in ordinary conversation would be the common locution for face-saving truth-telling: "Now don't get me wrong, but I am told that so-and-so said such-and-such about you." Unfortunately, the gesture seldom works. When injured, one always blames the messenger for the message. This was Moynihan's problem. He meant well, but he brought bad news, poorly expressed. Liebow brought the same news, with almost no controversy.

In *Tally's Corner,* Liebow puts himself right into the mix where he must be responsible for what is said no less than for what transpired.

> Sea Cat was changing his clothes preparatory to going out. I flopped on his bed to wait for him and a package of prophylactics fell out from under the mattress. In replacing it, I discovered a dozen or more similar packages. I asked Sea Cat if he always used them. He said no, sometimes he does, sometimes he doesn't. [p. 99]

There is little of the remote false familiarity of the participant observer in this. Liebow is not in Sea Cat's room to conduct a formal interview. If information were to come from the visit (as it did), it would come by the accident of their relationship. Though the language, as written here, is a bit on the formal side ("prophylactics" instead of "rubbers"), the action is intimate. Liebow "flopped" on the bed. When the condoms fell out, he felt no shame either in putting them away for Sea Cat or in asking about his use of them.

Liebow's query led to a most interesting response: "It depends on the girl. If she's nice," said Sea Cat, "the kind I wouldn't mind helping out, then I don't use them. But if she's not nice, I don't take any chances." [pp. 99] In 1967, the acronym HIV/AIDS was unknown. Schoolchildren did not practice putting condoms on bananas, as they do today. Condoms were about sexually transmitted disease. Sex was about sex. Birth control, for the nice girls in suburbs at least, involved the Pill. For Liebow to have been so thoroughly comfortable with Sea Cat as to handle his rubbers and ask about his sex, he had to have done some kind of extraordinary work as a member of the streetcorner action. The yield of that work, in this and other instances, is what to some readers must have been a weird reply. Sea Cat, it seems, reverses the middleclass sexual ethic in which an unwanted pregnancy is stigmatizing. The nice girl gets the straight sex: "If she's nice, the kind I wouldn't mind helping out, then I don't use them." The not-nice girl is a health hazard; hence, the condoms. The scene establishes not so much a blind intimacy as a distance, bridged by the talk of sex, between the apparently opposite sexual ethics of the middle classes and the street-corner man. Between the two, no judgment is made. One sparse footnote describes, without heavy interpretation, the distance between the sexual cultures. The story occurs more than halfway through the book, after the literary pattern has already settled in to good effect.

Familiarity of this kind is not at all unusual for an ethnographer. Today, Mitchell Duneier, another white author of books on the Black man[2], is famous for the ease with which he quickly forms friendships with the people others might think of as "informants." But familiarity can be a trap of its own kind—one that holds the ethnography in thrall to his private instincts, which in turn can repel him toward the extreme of an implausible objectivity. Hence, the bad reason for the ethnographer to distance himself is that of setting himself up as the authoritative author—as the one

---

2. Mitchell Duneier, *Slim's Table: Race, Respectability, and Masculinity* (Chicago: University of Chicago Press, 1992); and *Sidewalk* (New York: Farrar, Strauss & Giroux, 1999). Though Duneier has been criticized for having allowed familiarity to blind him to those he studies, many others admire the care with which, in *Sidewalk*, he has worked to use his gift for friendship in the service of ethnography.

who has seen the truth he now conveys to the reader. The duplicity derives from the Janus-like position the ethnographer assumes—intimate to the people, objective scientist to the reader of his writing. Too much of either and both faces are lost.

Liebow measures the familiarity against the social distance he retains, not just in his fieldwork, but also in the writing. This is a move vastly more subtle than getting in close with the people, to follow their every move and mention, in order to return to the world of science in the writing. Liebow broke new methodological ground by writing his way around the trap of ethnographic duplicity. He just tells the story. Though there are moments, like the account of Sea Cat's rubbers, when the reader may realize that Liebow's presence is motivated by his science, his literary genius is that the reader hardly ever is troubled by it—*evocative, not provocative*. It is one thing to trust, say, Faulkner in *Absalom, Absalom!* where the facts are not at issue. It is quite another to trust Liebow in *Tally's Corner* where, however much one wants the story to work, it cannot work for long unless the facts are right or at least right enough. Liebow's story, every bit as tragic as Faulkner's of the decline of the Sutpen and Coldfield families, works *as a story* because its telling invites a trust in the facts and realities of the place (social and geographic) on which it rests.

Literary effect requires that the local places be real enough to give the story plausibility. The authenticity of ethnography thus does not rest on the ability of the field-worker to write as the guide with the lamplight of scientific facts and categories. Instead, an ethnography rings true or not—and when true, it describes the people and places convincingly. Measured from the point of view of science, this is circular reasoning. But, for better or worse, *writings about people* can never be simply scientific. If they are, they fall flat. One need not overwork the ethnographic relation with the people as if to justify the truth of the writing about them. So long as their story is honestly told, they will speak for themselves either in so many words or in the subtext of the story. They simply have to be allowed to make themselves available to the reader. Beyond that, the less said the better. Sea Cat's sex life is convincing not because it is mine but because it puts mine in its own human place.

The scientific value of local place stories is in their ability to evoke in the reader a sense of plausible connectedness to some world they may not know firsthand. All a reader needs, at the point of reading (as opposed to criticism), is to be able to put himself into the picture, if only as an embarrassed stranger to the action. I first paused on the account of Sea Cat's rubbers when I remembered the first time, just at the onset of puberty, I saw a used condom on the street. I was walking with a friend, the wildest kid in the class. We both pretended not to know what that thing was. If that kid might blush, then I knew all I needed to know about rubbers. The plausibility of Liebow's easy conversation about Sea Cat's rubbers can rest on so thin a reed as the reader's realization that those dirty little things are something else. The mistake many ethnographers make is in trying to convince too much by showing just how close they were to the people or by offering data or categories that enlighten the story in the glow of science.

Tally's Corner reads less like a story of the truth of the lives of these men (though it can be taken that way) than of a moment in the lives of some men in a certain place—that is, a story so particular in its representations that the reader wants to transport himself into that place even though it can no longer exist for the visiting. Patricia Clough would say,[3] perhaps, that the writing is more like a movie than anything else. The story is not, of course, told in real time. The reader-observer is not so much expected to be or go there as to respect the unconscious desires that put him into the scene as the images are projected from behind in a darkened room that focuses attention on the not-there reality of the unfolding

---

3. Patricia Clough, *End(s) of Ethnography: From Realism to Social Criticism* (New York: Peter Lang, 1998).

story. As it always is with desires, the individual is caught in the between of the visible presence and the invisible absence of unconscious feeling.

This is not to say that *Tally's Corner* is perfect. No scientific book written some forty years before could be—especially not since those years of the last half of the twentieth century were the years when thinking in the social sciences underwent so many revolutions, of which intrigue with the narrative is one.[4] Still, what astonishes in Liebow's book is how plain but elegant the writing is. At no point is this unusual juxtaposition of qualities more evident than in the way the story is plotted so as to allow the drama to unfold quietly toward a conclusion that grows steadily in the readerly unconscious as the pages turn. How does this work?

First, consider that no one who would read this book, and especially no one who might have picked it up in the late 1960s, would have come to it without the question of the Black man of the city well in mind. From 1965, the year of the Moynihan report, on through the remainder of the calendrical decade, the 1960s were themselves the history of the evolving Black man in

---

4. Though I admire many ethnographies for different reasons, not even Judith Stacey's *Brave New World* (New York: Basic Books, 1990), which experiments with new ethnographic techniques, does this as well as Liebow. At the same time, one might say that Stacey and other feminist ethnographers were able to do what they did because of earlier work of the kind Liebow pioneered. Carol Stack's *All Our Kin* (New York: Harper & Row, 1974) was in many ways the feminist sequel to *Tally's Corner*. Very few have worked the path of influence and change from early community studies through feminist standpoint theory to the new ethnographies. The most brilliant work of this kind is by Audrey Sprenger, whose 2000 University of Wisconsin doctoral dissertation, "Place Maps the Sociology of the Family," will soon be published. Sprenger's work not only clarifies the uncertain relations between community ethnography and feminist theory but also is itself an ethnography of home stories in a remote industrial forest of Manitoba. No one has influenced my thinking about ethnographies, local places, and distancing more than Sprenger, who disagrees with my interpretation of *Tally's Corner* (notably in e-mail communications of February 2 and 7, 2003, among others). For my own understanding of Sprenger's work, see Charles Lemert, *Social Things* (Lanham, Md.: Rowman & Littlefield, 2002), chapter 11.

American consciousness. *Tally's Corner* begins with what, for the times, must have been read as a rather low-key statement of the crisis, then fresh in everyone's mind, of the poverty that afflicted Negroes in America's cities. Here is where reference is made to the extreme emphasis on the female-headed household (one of several indirect references to the furor over the Moynihan report). In simple language, Liebow states his intention to correct the emphasis. "The adult [Black] male, if not simply characterized as 'absent,' is depicted as a somewhat shadowy figure who drifts in and out of the lives of the family members."[5] [p. 3] After another section of introductory remarks on the sociology of the Black man of the city, Liebow takes a surprising turn. In addition to describing the corner where the New Deal Carry-out shop is the center of action, he introduces Tally, Sea Cat, Richard, and Leroy—the main men on the corner. We are told thereby that this story is about real men who have names and who can be described in real human terms.

"Men and Jobs" (chapter 2) begins with the story that had been coursing through public opinion of the time. It is morning. A pickup truck drives by the corner. The driver offers day work. The men on the corner look up to consider the day's pay. But none takes the offer. Up and down the street, as the work truck departs, men can be seen standing or sitting about. It is work time. A job is offered. The men stay put.

Could there be a better picture of the popular misconception of the Black man of the city? If today that picture is reshot in gangster colors, the negatives can be superimposed. The popular image of the Black man of the city is that he wants no part of this world of work and family. The first take is that Liebow is confirming the impression. But *Tally's Corner* immediately turns the story on itself. Using the accounts of Tonk, Richard, Leroy, and Sea Cat, Liebow

---

5. Note, for the time being, the use of the word "shadowy," which will bear an important literary weight as Liebow's own story of the Negro man unfolds.

describes the kind of work offered by those who come to the inner city early of a morning offering day labor. The work is usually back-breaking labor at construction, carrying hods of brick the day long. Even young men will lack the endurance to bear such loads. These men are not all that young. Even those able to bear the physical demands realize that the work is irregular according to season, weather, and the whim of employers seeking nonunion labor. The only regular work, when it is not some three or more hours' bus travel to the suburbs, is menial labor in restaurants, groceries, hotels, and the like (traditional employment for Black men who were not railway porters, and work that today is ever-farther removed from the inner city). The men decline the work because they know where it leads—nowhere!

Then, the key interpretation in the early going of *Tally's Corner*: "The streetcorner man puts no lower value on the job than does the larger society around him." [p. 36] These men are like any others. They know what it means to be the breadwinner, to bring home a paycheck that serves the needs of the family, to have a family, to be present to one's children and partners. In short, they are men in the modern and acutely American sense that manhood is personhood with responsibilities. "The desire to be a person in his own right, to be noticed by the world he lives in, is shared by each of the men on the streetcorner." [p. 38] As if to soften the formal language, in one of the longer passages from his field notes Liebow offers what might be called "Tally's Lament":

> "You know that boy came in last night? That Black Moozlem? That's what I ought to be doing. I ought to be in his place."
> "What do you mean?"
> "Dressed nice, going to [night] school, got a good job."
> "He's no better off than you, Tally. You make more than he does."
> "It's not the money. [Pause] It's position, I guess. . . . People respect him." [p. 38]

The better pay mentioned by Liebow was Tally's take from a seasonal job as a cement finisher. Liebow tries to talk Tally into feeling better about his life by glamorizing the cement work:

> "Nobody knows everything. One man is a doctor, so he talks about surgery. Another man is a teacher, so he talks about books. But doctors and teachers don't know anything about concrete. You're a cement finisher and that's your specialty." [p. 39]

With this, Tally concludes his lament: "Maybe so, but when was the last time you saw anybody standing around talking about concrete?"

You've got to admire both men—Tally for the honesty with which he understands his situation and describes it; Liebow for the honesty of revealing himself, in that one instance, as the liberal do-gooder, trying to talk the real man out of his well-structured fate. Another social scientist, one less confident than Liebow, might have carried on at inordinate length about the force and power of structures of the labor market. But Liebow merely alludes to the sociology of structures in a few footnotes. He prefers to let the story of "Men and Jobs" stand on its own—as the account, precisely, of the fate of the Black man of the socially structured city.

This one chapter sets up the story line as it unfolds in the next four chapters, each shorter by a good measure than "Men and Jobs." They are shorter, perhaps, because "Men and Jobs" has already set both the line and the beat of the tales they tell. The narrative line passes through the separated spheres of the lives of the men—as father, as husband, as lover, as friend. In each, they fail, disappointing themselves most of all. Against the narrative line, Liebow brings home the steady beat of failure followed by a quiet explanation. The story line itself is not Liebow's invention. The failure of the Black man of the city was, and is, well told in the superficial noise of popular opinion. The society at large asks, *Why are these men different? Why do they fail?* They, through Liebow, reply, *For good reason!* Though defeat is written over the faces and backs of the men, they respond with a depressed but sensible defiance. *We are not different!*

"Fathers without Children" (chapter 3) tells of the men's attachments to their children, their awareness of who they are, and, under certain conditions, their touching intimacies with them. But here the image is the reverse of the public one—an apparent contradiction that can be accounted for. The men who live *apart* from their children are more, not less, demonstrative with them. Those who live *en famille* are very often cold and indifferent to the children. Why? Very simply because, if they are living at home, they are publicly committed to their kids. They are, in short, in the visible role of the breadwinner. But, more likely than not, for want of decent jobs they are unable to meet the breadwinner demands. So to be in the home with the children is to have one's failure on display. Hence, the practice of distancing themselves from the children, or in Liebow's words, "saying, in effect, 'I'm not even trying to be your father so now I can't be blamed for failing to accomplish what I'm not trying to do.'" [p. 56] *Men without jobs are fathers without children.* In America, that is the way it is

"Husbands and Wives" (chapter 4) and "Lovers and Exploiters" (chapter 5) would appear on the surface to make a false distinction. But, once again, the appearance is what meets the eye of bourgeois public opinion. In the reality of the Black man of the city, the strain is most acute. *Men without jobs are fathers without children because they cannot be husbands to the mothers.* As a consequence, their relations with mothers of the children and other women in their lives are unstable because of the enormous pressure of failure before the demands of the wider culture that a real man be a good provider. In these two chapters the beat of the story quickens as the story becomes raw—not just with sex but also with the vain attempts of the men to account for their failure as fathers and husbands. Here Liebow introduces the theory of sexual infidelity as a manly flaw, offering his most robust theory of the *apparently* flawed manhood of the Black man of the city. In contrast to Tally's Lament on the emotional poverty of work as a cement man, we have here Sea Cat's Boast:

> Men are just dogs! We shouldn't call ourselves human, we're just dogs, dogs, dogs! They call me a dog, 'cause that's what I am, but so is everybody else—hopping around from woman to woman, just like a dog. [p. 78]

Liebow adds that the other street-corner men who were in earshot of Sea Cat's Boast nodded agreement. Here the deficits in self-esteem rise up in a different voice, one that is partly defensive, partly a reach for what honor can be had. They cannot be real men. They must be dogs. It's a theory, at least, a way of accounting for their situation. At least they are something.

Men without jobs are fathers without children because they cannot be husbands to the mothers because they are sexual dogs. The narrative logic comes clear. This is where (in "Lovers and Exploiters") Liebow tells the story of Sea Cat's condoms and sexual habits, the story that appears to reverse the middle-class norms. Sea Cat saves the rubbers not for the nice girls but for the not-nice ones. The logic is exactly parallel to their parental reasoning. One saves the affection for the kids one is separated from and denies it to those with whom one lives. In both cases, and throughout the story, the slowly emerging logic of these Black men of the city serves to defend, as best they can, against the assaults of an economic system that assures failure in all aspects of life. They use condoms—to protect themselves from disease that would still the dog within. They care for their children—when they can without admitting to their failure as men.

The story is far from happy. A lesser man than Liebow might have edited it or put a happy face on some aspect of it. But *Tally's Corner* contains not a word of condescension. In fact, the reader is aware throughout that the ethnographer looks beyond the behaviors of the men—behaviors the wider society condemns—to who they are. And he respects them for what they are and in spite of the fact that they are not respectable. Liebow pulls no punches. The distance he keeps from the men is the social space of his regard for them.

In the concluding chapters of the book, he returns to the beginning. In "Friends and Networks" (chapter 6), Liebow settles back into the unsettled corner society of the men. In one sense all they have is each other. Yet, even here what they have, they have not for long. Even the closest of relations among the men are vulnerable to the manly-flaws syndrome, most painfully in the story of Tally and Richard. The two had essentially passed as kin, about as tight as men could tie themselves to each other. But soon enough Richard felt that Tally had become the lover of his wife, Shirley. Nothing could dissuade Richard of this idea. The terrible consequence of the theory of manly flaws, when applied to oneself, is that those who think of themselves as sexual dogs cannot imagine that others, even their closest friends, are not also dogs. Tally had not had any intimate contact with Richard's wife. Still, they came near to blows over Richard's fear of Tally, which was, of course, a fear of himself. When one lacks all but the most rudimentary sense of self-esteem, he cannot sustain the requirements of life with others.

In the end (chapter 7), Liebow offers his own theory of the Black man of the city:

> Sometimes he sits down and cries at the humiliation of it all. Sometimes he strikes out at her or the children with his fists, perhaps to lay hollow claim to being man of the house in the one way left open to him, or perhaps simply to inflict pain on this woman who bears witness to his failure as a husband and father and therefore as a man. Increasingly he turns to the streetcorner where a shadow system of values constructed out of public fictions serves to accommodate just such men as he, permitting them to be men once again

provided they do not look too closely at one another's credentials. [p. 138]

We who read this from the perspective of time might find it all too familiar. But it is important to remember that the familiarity of this early story of the Black man of the city owes precisely to his emergence, over the decades since, at the center of American social consciousness. In 1967, there was no hip-hop, unless you count Muhammad Ali's rhyming, as some do.[6] In 1967, there were urban gangs, as there had been through the years, but the gangsta' had not become the legendary figure of street life. There was thus no talk of the code of the streets (of which Elijah Anderson writes)[7] and therefore no revisionist talk of the Black man as really more respectable than most people think (of which Mitchell Duneier writes).[8] Nor then was the urban ethnography of the Black man so much the center of social scientific debate as it is today.[9]

---

6. Charles Lemert, *Muhammad Ali: Trickster in the Culture of Irony* (Cambridge, UK: Polity Press, 2003).

7. Elijah Anderson, *The Code of the Street: Decency, Violence, and the Moral Life of the Inner City* (New York: W. W. Norton, 1999).

8. Duneier, *Slim's Table.* Duneier's subsequent book, *Sidewalk,* carries forth many of the same themes.

9. Duneier's views and Anderson's have been subjected to what is surely the longest and one of the most viciously brilliant review essays ever published in an academic journal: Loic Wacquant, "Scrutinizing the Street: Poverty, Morality, and the Pitfalls of Urban Ethnography," *American Journal of Sociology* 107: 6 (May 2002): 1468–32. Among Wacquant's points of assault against Anderson's code theory of the Black man of the city is that it too severely dichotomizes the Black man between the decent and the street codes. On the other hand, Wacquant excoriates Duneier for, among other reasons, naively romanticizing the Black men he studies. Curiously, in their responses to Wacquant (in the same issue of the *American Journal of Sociology*), neither Anderson nor Duneier is particularly convincing, in large part because neither they nor Wacquant take seriously Liebow's interpretation—that the men are both decent and street men, both longing for respectability and unable to achieve it. Wacquant, one supposes, would claim that Du Bois was just another American sociologist. He is surely right that, at the least, Duneier might have been more convincing to his critics had he taken on Du Bois's scheme. Anderson, it is true, may

In 1967, Liebow wrote very much on his own terms. Though he does not mention W. E. B. Du Bois's now famous concept of the double consciousness of the American Negro, one cannot help but believe that Du Bois's idea had somehow filtered down into Liebow's thinking. The shadow system of values is very much in keeping with the haunting words Du Bois used: "The history of the American Negro is the history of this strife,—this longing to attain self-conscious manhood, to merge his double self into a better and truer self."[10] What impresses the most is that Elliott Liebow chose his terms well, especially from a literary point of view.[11] To speak of a shadow value system is to speak of the wider society's hauntings of the consciousness and behaviors of those it oppresses. This is akin to Du Bois's disturbing figure of the veil of the color line in America. In both, the effects of racism come down on the individual indirectly—more through the unconscious of collective life than by overt choices.[12] That Tally can lament so self-consciously the social degradations of the cement finisher is in many

---

have invited the criticism Wacquant makes by using the semiotics of codes as his organizing figure. But Wacquant ignores for the most part Anderson's code switching idea, which has the effect of pointing to the ways practices are shaped into structurally organized and organizing dispositions.

10. W. E. B. Du Bois, *Souls of Black Folk* (1903; reprint, New York: Bantam Books, 1989), chapter 1. Also, if unbelievably, in 1967 Du Bois was scarcely read and certainly not widely discussed as he is today. This makes it all the more remarkable that his idea does not figure in the thinking of Wacquant and Duneier, though it clearly stands in the background of Anderson's code theory.

11. He refers to Hyman Rodman's "value stretch" theory as a source for the shadow values idea, even though stretching is hardly the right term. See Hyman Rodman, "The Lower-Class Value Stretch," *Social Forces* 42: 2 (December 1963): 205–15.

12. By contrast, the inflexibility of Anderson's code metaphor is such that when he tries to account for the double-consciousness of the street- and decency-encoded men and women, he must speak of code switching—a relatively rational decision. Also, it should be said that Robert K. Merton's classic 1938 essay, "Social Structure and Anomie," is quite explicitly in the background of Liebow's thinking. But Liebow, in fact, improves at the crucial point on Merton's scheme, which again leaves the adjustment to a structural dilemma to the more rational process of adaptation.

ways remarkable. But Liebow wants us to know that these are remarkable men—men who suffer the effects of a complex system that sneaks into their heads.

Some today would complain that the shadow value system explanation is a relatively weak psychology of the Black man of the city. But, as Loic Wacquant might say,[13] this is one of the pernicious influences of a distinctively American sociology whereby all actions are explained either by a psychology of the subject or by a sociology of objective structures. One might not claim for Elliott Liebow any particular status as a pioneer in the theory of social structures (in the United States, at least, the social theory of structures did not enter seriously into controversy until the decade following *Tally's Corner*). But one could insist that Liebow's theoretical instincts were superb. In fact, *Tally's Corner* is a story of the Black man of the city told from the point of view of social structures. The shadow values of these men are the consequences, not the cause, of their situation, and, before it is anything else, it is a situation that comes down to them in the mornings when the pickup trucks looking for day workers come to the street corner. They knew exactly where those day jobs were going, and they weren't buying it. The costs were too great for the impossibility of real human dignity.

This is one of the reasons William Julius Wilson's introduction to this edition of *Tally's Corner* is so filled with respect for Elliott Liebow. There could hardly be a sociologist better known than Wilson for his robust socioeconomic and structural analysis of the Black man of the city. Yet, Wilson does not shrink from considered attention to the effects of those larger structural forces at the interior of these men who are subjects subjugated by an urban political economy that, apart from its inherent racism, provides no dignified employment for the already poor Black man of the city.[14]

---

13. Wacquant, "Scrutinizing the Street," 1520–27.

14. Wilson himself has written on what some might call the social psychology of ghetto-related behavior in *When Work Disappears: The World of the New Urban Poor* (New York: Alfred Knopf, 1996), chapter 3. See also the excellent work of Alford

On margin, Liebow must be credited for having realized that it is impossible to study men in this circumstance by means of the enlightened gaze of the all-too-formal analytic categories of the social sciences. Yes, of course, he *saw* in the fieldwork what was happening to these men and how they understood themselves. But seeing is only the beginning of good ethnography. In fact, the best writing about people comes less from a clear vision into their secrets than from a keen inner ear for what they are saying behind what they are saying. The writer who believes too firmly in his visual acuity will pontificate. Liebow does not. He writes more from the ear, as one who trusts what he hears and thus is willing to write without the clumsy pretenses that too often deaden sociological writing. He chose not a hard and distinct analytic concept to account for these men but the haunting refrain of the shadows—the very shadows that both keep the Black men of the city in the dark and spook them into despair as to their very own worth.

The great value of a literary sensibility like Liebow's is that it allows the reader to enter the story, to form his own connection with the people, to see them in their differences from his own situation. *Tally's Corner* was not, of course, written by Tally and the other men. Nor was it written *for* them. It was written for the millions, as it turned out, who came to the book at the risk of implicating themselves. The story of the Black man of the city is ultimately the story of the modern city itself and, in turn, of the postmodern global economy. It is a story that is nowhere near its final chapter.

The most beautiful thing about Elliott Liebow's book is that he invites us across the extreme social distances into the lives of these men—men who no longer live as they once did on a street corner that can no longer be found. In this, he allows us, should we be as forthcoming as he was, to find our own places in a harshly structured system that leaves men like Tally so bereft of hope.

Young Jr. (who worked with Wilson in the Chicago studies) in *The Minds of Black Men: Making Sense of Mobility* (Princeton: Princeton University Press, 2003).

FOREWORD TO THE
1967 EDITION

Hylan Lewis

Elliot Liebow has written a sensitive and timely book about a shifting collection of anchorless adult Negro males who came together more or less regularly on Tally's Corner in a blighted section of Washington's inner city during the early 1960's. The Carry-out shop on Tally's Corner was a fixed spot around which their complex but limited lives eddied and flowed.

Carry-out shops, laundromats, and record shops have recently come to the ghetto in numbers. They join taverns, pool halls, liquor stores, corner groceries, rooming houses, secondhand stores, credit houses, pawn shops, industrial insurance companies, and storefront churches as parts of a distinctive complex of urban institutions that have undergone changes in adapting to the effective wants, limited choices, and mixed tastes of inner-city residents. Inner-city carry-out shops serve many functions other than selling prepared food. Among other things they may serve as informal communication centers, forums, places to display and assess talents, and staging areas for a wide range of activities, legal, illegal, and extralegal. And although they exist in the heart of the city, they are like outpost institutions—gathering places for outsiders in the center of the city.

The worsening of the ghetto-centered crisis in our cities has indicated that the critical problem for all of us now is, as Professor Nathan Keyfitz has pointed out, how to "cross simultaneously these coinciding lines"* of income, race, education, and residence which separate the poor from the middle class, particularly in our cities.

Much of this book is concerned with the acting, as well as classic acting-out behavior, and the varying levels of responses of these poor and marginally poor urban Negro males. To the extent that this is true, *Tally's Corner* is as akin in preoccupation and point to Ralph Ellison's fictional classic, *Invisible Man,* as it is to William Foote Whyte's sociological classic, *Street Corner Society*; and to Eugene O'Neill's *The Iceman Cometh* as it is to Kenneth B. Clark's *Dark Ghetto,* or Lee Rainwater's "Crucible of Identity: The Negro Lower Class Family."

The current relevance of this description of the adaptive habits and habitat of these Negro streetcorner men is related in part to something Dr. Liebow discovered for himself early in his field-work for the Child Rearing Study of the Health and Welfare Council of the National Capital Area. He became acutely aware of the manner in which relationships between Negroes and whites, the educated and the uneducated, the poor and the nonpoor are mixed up with roles and acting.

After a year of studying the men and women on and around Tally's Corner, Dr. Liebow wrote of "the chain-link fence [between us], since despite the barriers we were able to look at each other, walk alongside each other, talk, and occasionally touch fingers." And with respect and humility, he added "I used to play

---

*Nathan Keyfitz, "Privilege and Poverty: Two Worlds on One Planet," *Bulletin of the Atomic Scientists,* (March 1966).

with the idea that maybe I wasn't as much of an outsider as I thought. Other events, and later readings of the field materials, have disabused me of this particular touch of vanity."

More important than the awareness of barriers was the realization that the wavering lines between Elliot Liebow, white male, and the Negro males from around Tally's Corner were not related solely, and by no means simply, to racial differences. Differences in income, education, residence and temperament were also involved. And it is important to add that the interplay of stances and responses related to these factors made for equally as perplexing methodological and personal problems for William Watson, a Negro fieldworker simultaneously assigned to work with the same men and women in the same area for several months.

Dr. Liebow's penetrating analysis of the worlds of the street-corner men goes a long way toward accounting for the survival and resiliency of these men—but at what cost!—in the face of the disorganization, insecurity and the anti-community forces that converge on and operate within the contemporary urban slum. Like others under unrelenting stress and catastrophic conditions, these men fall back on the primary group; they use friendship and the "up-tight" buddy system as resource and buffer and in their design to protect dignity and to rationalize and conceal failure if necessary.

The adaptation of the streetcorner man has an atavistic, ad hoc, and fictional character about it. First, Liebow found the whole social structure of the streetcorner world resting to a large extent "on the primary, face-to-face relationships of the personal network." An important point that Liebow makes is that these relationships rest almost entirely in present time: "Friendship thus appears as a relationship between two people who, in an important sense, stand unrevealed to one another." The poignant paradox of Liebow's streetcorner men is that they live their daily lives within a complex web of recognition and nonrecognition, in spite of the necessity of having, or acting out friendship.

For these unanchored men, as for all men, friendship is a source of security and self-esteem. For streetcorner men with small stability and fewer options, there appear to be added incentives "to romanticize relationships, to upgrade them, to elevate what others see as a casual acquaintanceship to friendship, and friendship to close friendship. . . . It is as if friendship is an artifact of desire, a wish relationship, a private agreement between two people to act 'as if,' rather than a real relationship between persons."

Second, because the streetcorner provides a selected catalogue of meaningful others for men who are somewhat adrift, it helps some of them endure the experience or prospect of failure—at least temporarily. On the streetcorner, "failures are rationalized into phantom successes and weaknesses magically transformed into strengths." In many ways, the streetcorner man is a con man and faker. Much of his behavior is "his way of trying to achieve many of the goals and values of the larger society, of failing to do this, and of concealing his failure from others and from himself as best he can."

Characteristically, the streetcorner men described here by Dr. Liebow were "losers"; they were persons who were not going anywhere and they knew it. Seriously flawed or severely handicapped by lack of education and skills, and inadequate income, they moved about in a kind of traditionless limbo—in a social milieu between that of the relatively stable and upwardly mobile lower-middle-class workingmen, and that of the derelict and bum.

One of the important contributions of this study is that it goes far toward factoring out the Negro streetcorner man from other Negro urban types—both lower-class and middle-class. It goes far toward helping us understand the processes by which "losers" like these streetcorner men are generated as well as the atavistic ways in which some adjust. It does not tell us about—nor was it intended to—those Negro males who are in some measure "winners" or at least not "losers," yet, in the same way as these streetcorner men. Nor does it tell us directly about those Negro streetcorner men in

Watts, Chicago, Rochester, Cleveland, and other urban centers, whose atavistic behavior has not been so externally benign.

Although Dr. Liebow was not supposed to transcend the area of Tally's Corner, the methodology, insight, honesty and compassion with which he has described and interpreted these men and women helps us to understand all men who face the fact that they are "losers" or are likely to be—but who are not so lost that they abdicate completely the quest for dignity.

Dr. Liebow has given the men and women of Tally's Corner dignity by indicating that they are complex, not simple, and affirming of the best in our society, even though sometimes in a perverse fashion.

Hylan Lewis
Howard University
January 1967

INTRODUCTION TO THE 2003 EDITION

William Julius Wilson

The true mark of a classic book is whether it can withstand the test of time. Elliott Liebow wrote *Tally's Corner* in the mid-1960s, yet his arguments concerning the work experience and family life of black street-corner men in a Washington, D.C., ghetto still ring true today. Indeed, Liebow was perhaps the first scholar to place appropriate emphasis on the fact that ongoing lack of success in the labor market lowers one's self-confidence and gives rise to feelings of resignation that frequently result in a temporary, or even permanent, abandonment of the job search. "The most important fact is that a man who is able and willing to work cannot earn enough to support himself, his wife, and one or more children," declared Liebow. "A man's chances for working regularly are good only if he is willing to work for less than he can live on, sometimes not even then." [p. 32]

The jobs filled by the low-status black men in Liebow's study were sometimes monotonous and back breaking but mostly underpaid. Neither respect nor status is attached to such jobs, and they provide little or no opportunity for advancement. It should hardly be surprising therefore that, like others in this society, the street-corner man viewed such jobs with disdain. "He cannot do otherwise," stated Liebow. "He cannot draw from a job those social values which other people do not put into it." [p. 37] Understandably, the work histories of the street-corner men were erratic. Menial employment was readily available, and workers drifted from one undesirable job to the next.

However, if the job market prospects for low-skilled black men were bleak when Liebow conducted his field research in the early 1960s, they are even worse today. In the last three decades, low-skilled African American males have encountered greater difficulty gaining access to jobs, even menial jobs. Although employment and wages for all low-skilled workers improved during the economic boom period of the late 1990s and into 2000, at the time of this writing, the country is in a jobless recovery and experiencing economic stagnation. Jobless rates, especially those in the inner city, are on the rise once again. The ranks of street-corner men have swelled since the early 1970s and include a growing proportion of adult males who routinely work in and tolerate low-wage jobs when they are available (Wilson 1996).

What has caused the deterioration in the employment prospects of low-skilled black men since Liebow wrote *Tally's Corner*? Although blacks continue to confront racial barriers in the labor market, many inner-city African American workers have been victimized by the decreased relative demand for low-skilled labor. The computer revolution (i.e., the spread of new technologies) is displacing low-skilled workers and rewarding the more highly trained; and the growing internationalization of economic activity, including trade-liberalization policies, has increasingly pitted low-skilled workers in the United States against low-skilled workers around the world. These changes have benefited highly educated or highly skilled workers, while lower-skilled workers face the growing threat of eroding wages and job displacement (Katz 1996; Schwartzman 1997).

One of the legacies of historic racism in America is a disproportionate number of African American workers who are unskilled. Accordingly, the decreased relative demand for low-skilled labor has had a greater adverse impact on blacks than on whites. Whereas the number of skilled African Americans (including managers, professionals, and technicians) has markedly increased in the last few years, the proportion of those who are unskilled is still relatively large. Why? Because the black population, held back by the cumulative experiences of racial restrictions, was overwhelmingly unskilled as late as the mid–twentieth century (Schwartzman 1997).

Recent research into the urban labor market by the economist Harry Holzer (1996) demonstrates the magnitude of the problem. Based on a survey of three thousand employers in Atlanta, Boston, Detroit, and Los Angeles, Holzer reports that only 5 to 10 percent of the jobs in central-city areas for non–college graduates require very few cognitive skills or work credentials. A much greater premium is being placed on workers who have the basic skills of writing, reading, and performing arithmetic calculations and who also know how to operate a computer. Moreover, most employers in Holzer's study require a high school degree, job references, and particular kinds of work experience. Given the oversupply of unskilled workers relative to the number of low-skill jobs, many poorly trained and low-educated individuals experience difficulty landing jobs even in a strong local economy (Holzer 1996; Center on Budget and Policy Priorities 1996). This is especially true for men.

Today, most of the new jobs for workers with limited education and experience are in the service sector, which hires relatively more women. The movement of lower-skilled men into the growth sectors of the economy has been slow. For example, "the fraction of men who have moved into so-called pink-collar jobs like practical nursing or clerical work remains negligible" (Nasar 1994). Indeed, the striking gender differences in recent job growth are partly due to the large concentration of women in the expanding social service sector. Lower-educated women, unlike their male counterparts, are working more, not less, than in previous years. The employment patterns of lower-educated women, like those with higher training and education, reflect the growth of social service industries (Lerman and Rein forthcoming).

For inner-city black male workers, the problems created by the decreased relative demand for labor have been aggravated by negative employer attitudes. Interviews of a representative sample of Chicago-area employers by my research team in the late 1980s revealed that a substantial majority considered inner-city black males to be uneducated, uncooperative, unstable, or dishonest (Wilson 1996). For example, a suburban drugstore manager commented:

> It's unfortunate but, in my business I think overall [black men] tend to be known to be dishonest. I think that's too bad but that's the image they have . . . They're known to be lazy. They are [laughs]. I hate to tell you, but. It's all an image though. Whether they are or not, I don't know, but, it's an image that is perceived. (Interviewer: I see. How do you think that image was developed?) Respondent: Go look in the jails [laughs].

A suburban employer of an electrical services firm, concerned about theft, offered the following unique explanation for why he would not hire an inner-city black male:

> If you're in a white neighborhood . . . and you have a manufacturing firm and a ghetto person comes there to apply, it doesn't make any difference what color his skin is . . . if you know that's where he's from you know several things. One is that if you give him a job there, he's going to be unbelievably pressured to give information to his peer group in the ghetto . . . about the security system,

the comings and goings of what's of value there that we could rip off. He's not a crook. He wants no part of it. But he lives in an area where he may be physically or in danger of his life if he doesn't provide the information to the people that live around him. As a manager, I know that. And I'm not going to hire him because of that. I'm not discriminating against him because he's black, I'm discriminating against him because he has a problem that he's going to bring [it] to me. Now the fact that he is black and it happens that the people around him are black is only coincidental. In Warsaw they were Jews. They had the same problem.

A president of an inner-city manufacturing firm expressed a different reservation about employing black males from certain ghetto neighborhoods:

> If somebody gave me their address, uh, Cabrini Green I might unavoidably have some concerns.
>
> Interviewer: What would your concerns be?
>
> Respondent: That the poor guy probably would be frequently unable to get to work and . . . I probably would watch him more carefully even if it wasn't fair, than I would with somebody else.[1]

Such attitudes are classic examples of what economists call statistical discrimination: employers make general assumptions about inner-city black male workers and reach decisions based on those assumptions without reviewing systematically the qualifications of an individual applicant. The net effect is that many inner-city black male applicants are never given the opportunity to prove

---

1. Because of the prevalence of such attitudes, the lack of access to informal job networks is a notable problem for black males, as suggested by the following employer's comments to our interviewer: "All of a sudden, they take a look at a guy, and unless he's got an in, the reason why I hired this black kid the last time is cause my neighbor said to me, yeah I used him for a few [days], he's good, and I said, you know what, I'm going to take a chance. But it was a recommendation. But other than that, I've got a walk-in, and, who knows? And I think that for the most part, a guy sees a black man, he's a bit hesitant, because I don't know."

their qualifications on an individual level. Although it is true that some of these men eschew entry-level jobs because of the working conditions and low wages, as did some of the men in *Tally's Corner,* many others would readily accept such employment. Statistical discrimination, although representing elements of class bias against poor inner-city workers, is clearly a racial practice. Far more inner-city black males are effectively screened out of employment than Latino or white males applying for the same jobs (Wilson 1996).

Unfortunately, the negative effects of employer perceptions of inner-city black males have been compounded by the restructuring of the economy. The increasing shift to service industries has resulted in a greater demand for workers who can effectively serve and relate to the consumer. Unlike women and immigrants, who have recently expanded the labor pool in the low-wage service sector, many employers feel that inner-city black males lack such qualities, and their rejection in the labor market gradually grows over time.

Thus, because of the decreased relative demand for low-skilled labor, inner-city black males are forced to turn to the low-wage service sector for employment, where they compete, often unsuccessfully, with the growing number of female and immigrant workers. The more these men complain or manifest their job dissatisfaction, the less attractive they seem to employers. They therefore encounter greater discrimination when they search for employment and clash more often with supervisors when they are hired (Wilson 1996). Since the expressed feelings of many inner-city black males about their jobs and job prospects reflect their plummeting position in a changing economy (Wilson 1996), it is important to link attitudinal and other cultural traits with the opportunity structure. Among these cultural traits is the commitment to fatherhood.

Indeed, the lack of commitment to fatherhood among street-corner men is a cultural problem that grows out of restricted opportunities and constraints. This was true when Liebow wrote *Tally's Corner,* and it is even more true in the early twenty-first century. More specifically, many inner-city fathers today, even those who are not typically street-corner men, have low self-efficacy when it comes to fatherhood, whether they are willing to admit it or not. Included among the norms of fatherhood is the obligation to provide adequate and consistent material support for your family. Continuing lack of success in the labor market reduces the ability of many inner-city men to adequately support their children, which in turn lowers their self-confidence as providers and creates antagonistic relations with the mothers of their children. Convenient rationalizations, shared and reinforced by the men in these restrictive economic situations, emerge that reject the institution of marriage in ways that enhance, not diminish, their self-esteem. The outcome is a failure to meet the societal norms of fatherhood that is even more widespread than that reported by Liebow in *Tally's Corner.*

Programs that focus on the cultural problems pertaining to fatherhood without confronting the broader and more fundamental issue of restricted economic opportunities have limited chances to succeed. In my view the most effective fatherhood programs in the inner city will be those that address attitudes, norms, and behaviors in combination with local and national attempts to improve job prospects. Only then will fathers have a realistic chance to adequately care for their children and envision a better life for themselves. Given the perceptive analysis of fatherhood in *Tally's Corner,* if Elliot Liebow were alive today, I am sure he would agree.

REFERENCES

Center on Budget and Policy Priorities. 1996. "The Administration's $3 billion Jobs Proposal," Washington, D.C.

Holzer, Harry. 1996. *What Employers Want: Job Prospects for Less-Educated Workers.* New York: Russell Sage.

Katz, Lawrence. 1996. "Wage Subsidies for the Disadvantaged." Working paper 5679, National Bureau of Economic Research, Cambridge, Mass.

Lerman, Robert I., and Martin Rein. Forthcoming. *Social Service Employment: An International Perspective.* New York: Russell Sage.

Nasar, Sylvia. 1994. "The Men in Prime of Life Spend Less Time Working." *New York Times,* December 1.

Schwartzman, David. 1997. *Black Unemployment: Part of Unskilled Unemployment.* Westport, Conn.: Greenwood Press.

Wilson, William Julius. 1996. *When Work Disappears: The World of the New Urban Poor.* New York: Alfred A. Knopf.

ACKNOWLEDGMENTS

This book was originally written as a Ph.D. dissertation in anthropology for The Catholic University of America. The present version does not differ substantially from the original.

I collected most of the data on streetcorner men between January 1962 and July 1963 as a fieldworker for the research project, "Child Rearing Practices Among Low Income Families in the District of Columbia." The Child Rearing Study was carried out by the Health and Welfare Council of the National Capital Area under a grant (OM-278) from the National Institute of Mental Health. Dr. Hylan Lewis was the director of the project. It was his idea and his decision to include streetcorner men as a subject of direct investigation. I am indebted to him for the opportunity to work on this phase of the Child Rearing Study and for the many insights into the low-income world that I gained from him.

I am also indebted to members of the Department of Anthropology, The Catholic University of America: to my major professor, Dr. Gottfried Lang, for his time, counsel, guidance and encouragement; and to Professors Regina Flannery Herzfeld, Michael Kenny and Jasper Ingersoll for their constructive theoretical and methodological suggestions as well as for their critical readings of the various drafts of the manuscript.

Dr. Robert Shellow, Chief of the Adolescent Process Section, Mental Health Study Center, gave generously of his time and knowledge. His encouragement and criticism have left me deeply indebted to him. I owe him much more than he suspects. I am also indebted to Dr. Stephen T. Boggs of the American Anthropological Association for his helpful suggestions while I was in the beginning stages of analysis and writing.

Many other persons were helpful in many different ways. I especially want to thank Dr. Joan Snyder, Dr. Harold Goldsmith, Mr. Derek Roemer, Mr. William Watson, Dr. Milton Shore, Dr. Thomas Gladwin, and Dr. James Osberg.

My chief debt, of course, is to the streetcorner men themselves and to their women and children. Unfortunately, pseudonyms had to be used throughout to protect their anonymity but they themselves know who they are and I thank them.

Nothing at all of what appears in this study should be construed as representing the interpretations, judgments or policies of any institution or any person other than myself.

Elliot Liebow
Adelphi, Maryland
April 1966

1

INTRODUCTION

Problems faced by and generated by low-income urban populations in general and low-income urban Negroes in particular
have become one of the chief concerns of the nation. We have
declared War on Poverty and mobilized public and private resources for a concerted effort to expunge delinquency and dependency from our national life.

This concern with poor people is nothing new. For more than
a century, private charities and occasionally state agencies have
been attempting to provide aid and comfort to the casualties of our
social and economic system. In the 1930's, the number of casualties precipitated by the depression visibly demonstrated the inability of existing charities to deal with the problem; social justice and
individual rights were redefined to enable certain segments of the
poor—especially the aged, the handicapped, widows, and children—to obtain relief as a matter of right rather than as a matter
of charity.

Spurred by a combination of swift population growth, techno-
logical advancement, and migration to cities, the number of the
poor and their problems have grown steadily since World War II.

In 1963, the poor constituted one-fourth of our total population. About 30 percent of the poor were Negroes.[1]

Public interest in poverty tends to focus on Negroes for good reasons. A large proportion of the poor are Negroes and, more important, an even larger proportion of Negroes are poor. Moreover, Negroes in poverty tend to be poorer than their white counterparts and tend more to remain in poverty over generations, so that poverty, like skin color, appears as a hereditary characteristic as well as a circumstance of social and economic life. The transmission of the life style of poverty from generation to generation has logically drawn attention to Negro family life as the context in which this transmission is assumed to occur. To a large extent, the Negro family has become the very model of the dependent, lower-class urban family and a primary target of policy makers and programmers in the war against poverty.

Much of what we know of Negro families in poverty, however, has been biased by an emphasis on women and children and a corresponding neglect of adult males. Neglect of the lower-class male is a direct reflection of his characteristic "absence" from the household, leaving behind him the "female-based" or "female-centered" household consisting of one or two generations of women and their dependent children. One result of his absence is that family studies among low-income urban groups tend to deal with "female-centered" households, so that one comes away with

---

1. These figures are based on one of the more conservative definitions of poverty: to live outside of poverty, the average family of four persons requires about 70 cents a day per person for food and $1.40 a day per person for everything else (1963 prices), or a total family income of $60 a week. Mollie Orshansky, "Counting the Poor: Another Look at the Poverty Profile." This article offers an excellent discussion of the statistics and definitions of poverty. [*Publisher's note:* For an update on the consumer price index and inflation rates through 2003, consult http://woodrow.mpls .frb.fed.us/research/data/us/calc/.]

To avoid repetition, I am throughout presenting footnote references with the name of the authors and titles only. See References (pp. 167–170) for full publication information on all works cited.

a picture of the low-income urban world as one peopled mainly with women and children. The adult male, if not simply characterized as "absent," is depicted as a somewhat shadowy figure who drifts in and out of the lives of the family members.

Neglect of the adult male as a subject of research into lower-class life is also furthered by middle-class concerns with delinquency and dependency, for these are the aspects of poverty which touch most directly on middle-class life; the one threatens the property, peace and good order of society at large; the other drains its purse. But research on delinquency and dependency usually deals only incidentally with men. Delinquency usually refers to juvenile behavior and thereby, by definition, excludes the adult male. Similarly, dependency is a status normally reserved for women and children. It typically excludes the able-bodied male adult who is seen as not needing or not deserving societal support.

This focus on young people and children in dealing with delinquency and dependency is strongly supported by the high affective value placed on children in our society and by the growing conviction on the part of those committed to breaking into "the cycle of poverty" that childhood is the place to attempt it. It is commonly assumed that it is too late to do anything about the values, goals and life styles of adults but that there is still time, perhaps, to effect a change in children whose ways of thinking and behaving have not yet settled into the traditional mold prescribed by their parents or by the conditions of lower-class life.

At the purely practical level, the lower-class Negro man is neglected from a research point of view simply because he is more difficult to reach than women, youths and children. He is no more at home to the researcher than he is to the case worker or the census taker.[2] And apart, perhaps, from his contacts with the police, he is less likely than women and children to come to the attention of the authorities. It is the youth or the child who attracts the se-

---

2. .See note 12, pp. 11–12.

lective concern of the school system, of social workers, of health workers, probation officers and other custodial agents; and it is the woman who, acting on behalf of herself and her children, allows herself to come under the scrutiny of welfare agencies and other institutions, for it is only by exposing herself that she can lay claim to the proffered goods and services.

Whatever the relative number of men, women and children who come to the attention of the authorities, the fact is that much of what we know about lower-class life is derived from those who do. This has important consequences for both research and public action. It not only tends to reinforce what is already perhaps an undue preoccupation of the general public with delinquency and dependency, but it also tends to focus on the carriers of delinquency and dependency to the relative neglect of the contexts in which delinquency and dependency occur.

Moreover, dealing exclusively or even principally with those who are most visible and accessible raises important questions of methodology and analysis quite apart from the question of the representativeness of the informants or the respondents: when the school dropout, the felon, the abandoned child, or the mother applying for Aid to Dependent Children comes to the attention of the authorities and becomes an object of social science research, he is, in a real sense, a captive informant in a captive and alien environment.

Thus, the need to expand the range of research into lower-class life is clear.[3] But there are other problems as well. There is, for example, a growing uneasiness about the validity of much of

---

3. Muzafer and Carolyn Sherif, for example, in "Youth in Their Groups in Different Settings," point out that "we have ample theory about 'delinquent subcultures' with very little bearing on the people who are their bearers or what happens to any of them, except those caught by the net of official statistics," pp. 38–39. In discussing the difficulty of arriving at suitable criteria for defining "lower class," S. M. Miller says that "we lack basic data on the poor and the economically and familially unstable" ("The American Lower Classes: A Typological Approach," p. 5).

the data already gathered, especially data gathered by interview and questionnaire. Appeals for data in depth go hand in hand with a widespread suspicion that lower-class persons are less tractable to interview and questionnaire techniques than are persons in the middle and upper strata. Thus Cohen and Hodges,[4] in assessing their own conclusions on characteristics of the LL (lower-lower) class, warn: "It is possible that interview and questionnaire techniques are more likely, when applied to LL respondents than when applied to respondents of other strata, to produce caricatures in which the halftones and shadings, present in the subject, are obliterated in the image."

The present study is an attempt to meet the need for recording and interpreting lower-class life of ordinary people, on their grounds and on their terms. The data to be reported and analyzed were originally collected by me as part of a larger five-year study, "Child Rearing Practices Among Low Income Families in Washington, D.C.," carried out by the Health and Welfare Council of the National Capital Area under a grant from the National Institute of Mental Health. Dr. Hylan Lewis, project director of the study, laid down no hard and fast rules for gathering the material, but the broad outlines and the focus were clear. The data were

---

4. Albert K Cohen and Harold Hodges, Jr., "Characteristics of the Lower-Blue-Collar-Class," p. 333. John Rohrer and Munro Edmonson express similar misgivings about their interviews: "We have noted, too, but even more helplessly, the difficulty of drawing lower class people into the net of middle class participation that our interviews necessarily involved" (*The Eighth Generation: Cultures and Personalities of New Orleans Negroes*, p. 309). S. M. Miller and Frank Reissman point out the dangers involved in assuming that a given response has the same meaning for a lower-class respondent as for a middle-class respondent ("The Working Class Subculture: A New View," p. 92). On this point see also Oscar Lewis, *The Children of Sanchez*, p. xxvii. Hylan Lewis asserts the value of the interview but adds that "the structured one-shot interview does not give us some of the kinds of information that we sorely need [in low income family research]. . . . Right now . . . there is a crying need to be aware of—and to try to record and interpret—the complexity, change and variability in [low income] family life and organization" ("Discussion of [Marion R. Yarrow's] 'Problems of Methods in Family Studies,'" p. 4).

to be collected by participant observation rather than by means of questionnaires or structured interviews. They were to be collected with the aim of gaining a clear, firsthand picture of lower-class Negro men—especially "streetcorner" Negroes—rather than of testing specific hypotheses. The focus was on the man as father, husband or other family member, but there were, by design, no firm presumptions of what was or was not relevant. In this sense, there was no detailed research design; the intention was frankly exploratory.

The data were collected during twelve months of intensive participant observation in 1962 and on a more intermittent basis through the first six months of 1963.[5] They span the four seasons of the year and all hours of the day and night.

The great bulk of the material is drawn from two dozen Negro men who share a corner in Washington's Second Precinct as a base of operations. These men are unskilled construction workers, casual day laborers, menial workers in retailing or in the service trades, or are unemployed. They range in age from the early twenties to the middle forties. Some are single, some married men; some of the latter are living with their wives and children, some not.

The main body of the data comprises a record of the day-by-day routines of these men as they frequented the streetcorner, the alleys, hallways, poolrooms, beer joints and private houses in the immediate neighborhood. Frequently, however, associations which began on the streetcorner led me out of the neighborhood to courtrooms, jails, hospitals, dance halls, beaches and private houses elsewhere in Washington and in Maryland and Virginia.

Since the data do not have "sense" built into them—that is,

---

5. The period of my association with the Child Rearing Study. Personal relationships established in the field, however, did not all end when my connection with the Child Rearing Study ended. Several are in force as of this writing. I have drawn freely on these ongoing relationships for specific examples as well as used them to gain a long-range perspective.

they were not collected to test specific hypotheses nor with any firm presumptions of relevance—the present analysis is an attempt to make sense of them after the fact.[6] I have taken as the framework for the presentation and analysis of the data the streetcorner man as breadwinner, father, husband, lover and friend. The simplicity of such a framework is one of its principal advantages. Another and perhaps more important advantage is that the materials fall quite easily, almost naturally, into such a framework. This "natural" fit grows out of the fact that in looking at the men as fathers, husbands, lovers, breadwinners, and so forth, we look at them in much the same way they look at themselves. Whether or not we are here dealing with cultural universals, we do have, in these categories of behavior, roles which are commonly recognized in our society, among the lower classes no less than among persons of higher socioeconomic status. Admittedly, the kinds of behavior which go into one or another of these roles may differ from class to class or within a class but the role labels—that is, the way in which behaviors are categorized—are essentially the same.[7]

---

6. This procedure, in which "the observations are at hand and the interpretations are subsequently applied to the data," Robert K. Merton calls "*post factum* sociological interpretations." Such explanations, he says, "remain at the level of *plausibility* (low evidential value) rather than leading to 'compelling evidence' (a high degree of confirmation)," and "The documentary evidence merely illustrates rather than tests the theory" (*Social Theory and Social Structure*, pp. 93–95). It could be argued, I believe, that the timing of hypothesis formulation is irrelevant; that regardless of whether hypotheses are generated *pre* or *post factum,* the test of their validity always rests on future replication; and that the only proper restriction on the generation of hypotheses or explanations is that they fit the data. Even assuming the correctness of Merton's position—it is, after all, a plausible argument—my own feeling is that, given the present state of the art, we can ill afford to look "merely plausible" explanations of human behavior in the mouth. For excellent discussions of this problem, see Herbert J. Gans, *The Urban Villagers*, pp. 347–348, and Howard S. Becker, "Problems of Inference and Proof in Participant-Observation."

7. The importance of role labels or role names ("father," "lover") is emphasized by S. F. Nadel: ". . . it will often be the names current in a society for different classes or types of persons which first suggest to us the existence of the respective roles" (*The Theory of Social Structure*, p. 33).

In a sense, organizing the materials around father-child, husband-wife, and friend and lover relationships is one of the ways in which the men themselves might organize them. Taking this inside point of view makes it easier to avoid structuring the materials in ways that might be alien to the material itself.

Still another advantage derives from this kind of framework. By organizing the materials around roles and relationships commonly recognized elsewhere in our society, the product should lend itself to direct comparison with similar models drawn from middle-class behavior or from other segments of the lower class.

There is no attempt here to describe any Negro men other than those with whom I was in direct, immediate association. To what extent this descriptive and interpretive material is applicable to Negro streetcorner men elsewhere in the city or in other cities, or to lower-class men generally in this or any other society, is a matter for further and later study. This is not to suggest, however, that we are here dealing with unique or even distinctive persons and relationships. Indeed, the weight of the evidence is in the other direction. True, neither the men nor the community were selected for representativeness by random sampling or other sophisticated selection techniques. In fact, they were not consciously selected at all; the focus on these particular men at this particular place came about, in large part, through accident.[8] It is important to keep in mind, however, that this "accident" did not take place on the moon or in the Philippines or some small rural community in North Dakota; it took place in the center of a major American city, in the heart of a Negro slum area, on a corner where men can be seen lounging all hours of the day and many hours of the night.

There is, to the eye of the observer, nothing distinctive about these men or this corner. The view is not much different a block or two away in any direction, in other sections of the city, or in the larger northern metropolitan areas. Gross structural and cul-

---

8. See Appendix: "A Field Experience in Retrospect."

tural features of daily life in this particular neighborhood bear a strong resemblance to those reported for the urban poor—and especially the urban Negro poor—in other parts of the country. Female-based households are conspicuously numerous. "Serial monogamy" appears as an important form of marriage. Men, women and children spend much of their time on the street, on corners, sitting "on the front," or leaning out of windows. Women frequently appear in public with their hair in curlers, wearing open-toed sandals or bedroom slippers. Juke-boxes, phonographs and radios pump the sounds of music everywhere. Lovemaking, mate seeking, gambling and drinking are important foci of adult life. "Trouble," "thrill," "fate" and "fall" (fear of falling still further down the social scale) appear as "major themes or motifs . . . areas and issues of general persistent and emotionally significant concern." [9]

The present attempt, then, is not aimed directly at developing generalizations about lower-class life from one particular segment of the lower class at a particular time and place but rather to examine this one segment in miniature, to attempt to make sense of what was seen and heard, and to offer this explanation to others. Hopefully, someone will find merit in one or another of the ideas (none of which may be new but all of which are original in the sense that they arose from this particular study) and test them systematically for their validity and their range of applicability. The

---

9. These characteristics have been selected from Walter Miller, "Cultural Features of An Urban Lower Class Community." Miller defines the "female-based" household as "one in which a male acting in the 'father' role is either absent from the household, only sporadically present, or when present, only minimally or inconsistently involved in the support and raising of children. It usually consists of one or more females of child-bearing age, frequently related . . . by blood or marriage ties, and often includes two or more generations of women; e.g., the mother and/or aunt of the principal child-bearing female." He defines the "serial monogamy" marriage pattern as one in which "a woman of child-bearing age has a succession of temporary mates, ranging from two to six or more, during her procreative years," p. 13, note. See also Miller's, "Implications of Urban Lower-Class Culture for Social Work."

concluding chapter may appear to belie this intent by including, besides a summary statement, speculation and general statements about Negro-white relations in our society.

The New Deal Carry-out shop is on a corner in downtown Washington, D.C.[10] It would be within walking distance of the White House, the Smithsonian Institution, and other major public buildings of the nation's capital, if anyone cared to walk there, but no one ever does. Across the street from the Carry-out is a liquor store. The other two corners of the intersection are occupied by a dry cleaning and shoe repair store and a wholesale plumbing supplies showroom and warehouse.

Walking north from the Carry-out shop for three blocks or more, one passes a fairly even mixture of dwelling units (generally old, three-story, red-brick row houses, most of them long since converted to rooming and tenement houses), an occasional apartment house, and small-business establishments such as liquor stores, grocery stores, barber shops, cleaners, launderettes, beauty parlors, poolrooms, beer joints, carry-out shops, pawnbrokers, and others. The incidence of residential units is highest in the middle of the blocks and tends to diminish as one approaches the corners where the businesses take over.

The cross streets in the immediate area are almost entirely residential. Here, too, are three-story, brick row houses and an occasional apartment house, but one also finds, here and there, a corner grocery, a steeple church or a storefront church, a parking lot, a funeral parlor, or some light commercial enterprise. One block

---

10. Washington, D.C. has long been one of the principal stopping-off places for Negroes moving up the Eastern seaboard out of Alabama, Georgia, the Carolinas and Virginia. In 1963, it was the only major city in the country with more Negroes than whites living in it. The 1962 population was 791,900; of these, 452,200 were non-whites. These figures apply to the resident population. On weekday mornings, the city and the surrounding Maryland and Virginia suburbs enter into a population exchange. The city gives up Negro women to the suburbs where they work as domestics, and receives, in exchange, white white-collar men. At the end of the workday, city and suburbs reclaim their own.

south of the Carry-out is a broad avenue which serves roughly to divide the Carry-out neighborhood from the downtown business and shopping district.

The residents in the Carry-out neighborhood are almost all Negroes. From census reports and other public sources the casual observer could easily confirm his impression that this is an area with a high incidence of crowded living quarters, poverty, crime, child neglect, and dependence. This particular area, for example, held first position in the Health and Welfare Council's *1960 Index of Social and Economic Deprivation of Neighborhoods in the District of Columbia*. It had the highest rate of persons receiving public assistance; the highest rate of illegitimate live births; the highest rate of births not receiving prenatal care; the second highest rate of persons eligible for surplus food; and the third highest rate of applicants eligible for medical assistance.

Not everyone, however, is poor, dependent, delinquent,[11] nor are all men in the area to be found, at one time or another, hanging out on the corner or in a beer joint, poolroom or hallway. The man who lives up the street from the Carry-out and works two or three jobs to keep his home and family together may divide all his waking time between home and job. Such a man may be unknown at the Carry-out and at other public places in the area.[12]

---

11. Many are, but many are not. Living conditions, for example, cover a wide spectrum: at one end is a family of eleven, including seven children, all enuretic, living in one room and sleeping in one bed, one cot, and on the floor; at the other end is a self-supporting family of four in an immaculate three-bedroom apartment whose windows boast flowered curtains and where, in the living room, a canary competes with a hi-fi set. The range is great but heavily weighted toward the overcrowded, broken-plaster end of the scale.

12. This study, therefore, offers a biased view of the men in the Carry-out area since it ignores those who are invisible from the vantage point of the streetcorner. It is difficult to say how many such men there are, but that there are some, I know, from having met them. My impression is that there are more such men than is commonly assumed but fewer than one might be led to expect from census reports. In census reports, the proportion of stable workers and family men tends to be overrepresented because their underemployed, less stable streetcorner counterparts are fre-

The Carry-out shop is open seven days a week. Two shifts of two waitresses spend most of their time pouring coffee, opening bottles of soda, and fixing hamburgers, french fries, hot dogs, "half-smokes" and "submarines" for men, women and children.[13] The food is taken out or eaten standing up because there is no place to sit down. But in the 10′ × 12′ customer area, there is wall space and other leaning facilities which lend themselves nicely to the Carry-out's business and social functions. On top of the cigarette machine or on the jukebox, for example, Bumdoodle, the Carry-out's numbers man in residence, conducts his business dealings with the white numbers backer who comes by daily to settle accounts with him and with other numbers men from the neighborhood.

For those who hang out there, the Carry-out offers a wide array of sounds, sights, smells, tastes, and tactile experiences which titillate and sometimes assault the five senses. The air is warmed by

---

quently not counted. Thus a Department of Labor report on the Negro family (the Moynihan Report) states flatly that many (low-income) Negro men "are just not there when the census enumerator comes around." The report notes that "Donald Bogue and his associates, who have studied the Federal count of the Negro man, place the error as high as 19.8 percent at age 28" ("The Negro Family: The Case for National Action," p. 43).

13. On weekdays, the Carry-out is open from eight in the morning until midnight; on Friday and Saturday nights, until 4 A.M. On Sundays it does not open until two in the afternoon. In addition to hamburgers and hot dogs, hot (canned) soups are also available, as are fried fish sandwiches and a variety of cold cuts. On weekends (Friday is a common payday) and on the days immediately following delivery of ADC and Social Security checks, people who have been eating hamburgers and "half-smokes" sometimes switch to pork chop or steak sandwiches. Evenings, there is an occasional call for a box of seafood or fried chicken. One can also get ice cream, candy, a pickled pig's foot, Fritos, pork skins, chewing gum or chewing tobacco, and B.C. and Stanback Headache Powders. For those who miss the 9 P.M. closing of the nearby Safeway (and Sundays, too), there is bread, milk, some staple canned goods, toilet paper, sanitary napkins, laundry soap, starch and other sundries. Regular laundry starch, incidentally, is probably purchased for eating as often as for laundry purposes. To the best of my knowledge, only women eat starch. A pregnant woman may eat as many as four or five boxes of Argo Gloss Starch in one day.

smells from the coffee urns and grill and thickened with fat from the deep-fry basket. The jukebox offers up a wide variety of frenetic and lazy rhythms. The pinball machine is a standing challenge to one's manipulative skill or ability to will the ball into one or another hole. Flashing lights, bells and buzzers report progress or announce failure. Colorful signs exhort customers to drink Royal Crown Cola and eat Bond Bread. On the wall, above the telephone, a long-legged blonde in shorts and halter smiles a fixed, wet-lipped smile of unutterable delight at her Chesterfield cigarette, her visage unmarred by a mustache or scribbled obscenities. In the background, a sleek ocean liner rides a flat blue sea to an unknown destination.

In this setting, and on the broad corner sidewalk in front of it, some twenty men who live in the area regularly come together for "effortless sociability."[14] They are not, in any strict sense, a group. No more than eight or ten, and usually fewer, are there at any one time. There is nothing to join, no obligations, no one to say whether you belong or do not belong. Some of the men have never spoken to some of the others beyond exchanging a casual greeting. Some are close friends, some do not like others, and still others consider themselves enemies. But each man comes here mainly because he knows others will be here, too. He comes to eat and drink, to enjoy easy talk, to learn what has been going on, to horse around, to look at women and banter with them, to see "what's happening" and to pass the time.

Tally—Tally is a brown-skinned man, thirty-one years old. He is six feet tall and weighs just under two hundred pounds. His size and carriage lend credibility to the general belief that he was once a professional heavyweight fighter. When asked to affirm or deny this status, Tally merely grins, assumes the classic stance of the boxer, and invites the questioner to "come on." No one does.

---

14. This beautifully descriptive term is taken from Josephine Klein, *Samples from English Cultures*, Vol. 1, p. 142.

Tally was born in Atlanta, Georgia. His sixty-year-old mother lives there now. Tally's father left the family within months after Tally was born. Tally never went to school. When he was eleven years old, he began working regularly for wages at such jobs as cleaning up a doctor's once and as dishwasher in a restaurant. Tally spent most of his teen years in Atlanta, and then, despite his inability to read or write, went into the army.

Tally came to Washington, D.C. in 1954. His first job here was as a cook in a hospital, but he later got a job as a laborer in construction work. Since 1959 he has been a semiskilled construction worker averaging about one hundred dollars a week in take-home pay for the six or seven months of the year in which he works regularly.

Tally moved into a room in the Carry-out area in the winter of 1961. In the eight years he has been in Washington, Tally has lived in the Northeast, Southeast, and Northwest sections of the city. During this same period, he has married and separated and fathered eight children, three with his wife and five others with five different women.

Sea Cat—Sea Cat is twenty-seven years old. He was born and raised in the Carry-out neighborhood and except for his army service has lived all his life in that area. Sea Cat quit school in the tenth grade. He got married when he was twenty but he has long been separated from his wife and children.[15] Sea Cat is of average height and weight. His large white teeth contrast sharply with his dark skin and his long, thick, processed hair. There is an air of excitement about Sea Cat. He moves with the easy grace of the athlete, and his sure, quick hands are almost always in evidence, whether he is throwing a ball or a stone around, telling a story with elaborate hand gestures or playing the pinball machine, which he dominates almost effortlessly. An excellent storyteller,

---

15. One of his two children died during the course of this study. See p. 103.

Sea Cat holds his audience as much by his performance as by the content of what he has to say. If he reports that "an old man was walking down the street," his body suddenly sags with the weight of age and his hands tremble and knees almost buckle as he becomes, for that moment, an old man walking down the street. If he reports that someone shouted something, he shouts that something.

Sea Cat disdains the ordinary, frequently choosing to see a special quality, talent or property in ordinary people and ordinary events. He looks at the world much like the caricaturist or the expressionist painter. By a carefully controlled distortion of reality as it is perceived by others—by hyperbole or fancy—he seeks out the individuality, the special character, of the men, women, and events around him.

Richard—Richard is twenty-four years old. He is about 5'10", thin and muscular. Richard was born and raised in a small town in the Carolinas. He graduated from high school and married a girl who had lived across the street from him since childhood. In 1960 Richard had to leave his hometown suddenly, in the middle of the night, after assaulting (with provocation, according to his own and his family's account) a local white policeman. His pregnant wife and their small son joined him in Washington a few days later.

Richard worked primarily at janitorial jobs but occasionally tried other kinds of work as well. In his first several months in the Carry-out area, Richard built a reputation for himself as a hardworking man who tried to do his best for his family and as an all-around nice guy. But as time wore on, things changed. Richard got into several fights. In one, he killed a man.[16] People grew afraid of Richard and began to avoid him. Richard dated his troubles from the killing, but they had, in fact, started long, long before.

---

16. See p. 110.

Leroy—Leroy is twenty-three years old. He is tall and thin, even thinner than Richard, and somewhat lighter skinned than most of the men in the area.

Leroy was an only child. He was born in the South but was raised from early infancy by his maternal grandmother in Chicago. He left high school in his last year and went into the navy. He was by far the most able of all the men in dealing with the written word.

Leroy came to the Carry-out neighborhood in the fall of 1961, immediately after his discharge from the navy. He had previously spent a few weekend leaves there with a navy friend whose family lived near the Carry-out. Leroy had never intended to remain in Washington, but somehow, after spending his mustering-out pay, he never got around to going "home," although he always talked of doing so, even after marriage and two children.

Most of Leroy's jobs had to do with hotels and parking lots. Most men and women liked Leroy well enough but he was generally considered weak and immature, a "boy" who "talked big" and who, when competing with men, women, or a job, would probably back down before the confrontation or be the loser after it.

SOME OF THE OTHER MEN

name	age	usual employment
Arthur	28	laborer
Boley	21	janitor
Budder	45	laborer
Clarence	30	laborer
Earl	22	laborer
John	29	counterman
Lonny	26	stock clerk—delivery
Preston	38	laborer

Robert	27	janitor
Stanton	44	truck driver
Stoopy	27	busboy—dishwasher
Sweets	26	busboy—dishwasher
Tonk	23	parking-lot attendant
Wee Tom	37	laborer
Wesley	21	retail delivery
William	31	truck driver

2

MEN AND JOBS

A pickup truck drives slowly down the street. The truck stops as it comes abreast of a man sitting on a cast-iron porch and the white driver calls out, asking if the man wants a day's work. The man shakes his head and the truck moves on up the block, stopping again whenever idling men come within calling distance of the driver. At the Carry-out corner, five men debate the question briefly and shake their heads no to the truck. The truck turns the corner and repeats the same performance up the next street. In the distance, one can see one man, then another, climb into the back of the truck and sit down. In starts and stops, the truck finally disappears.

What is it we have witnessed here? A labor scavenger rebuffed by his would-be prey? Lazy, irresponsible men turning down an honest day's pay for an honest day's work? Or a more complex phenomenon marking the intersection of economic forces, social values and individual states of mind and body?

Let us look again at the driver of the truck. He has been able to recruit only two or three men from each twenty or fifty he contacts. To him, it is clear that the others simply do not choose to work. Singly or in groups, belly-empty or belly-full, sullen or gregarious, drunk or sober, they confirm what he has read, heard and knows from his own experience: these men wouldn't take a job if it were handed to them on a platter.[1]

Quite apart from the question of whether or not this is true of some of the men he sees on the street, it is clearly not true of all of them. If it were, he would not have come here in the first place; or having come, he would have left with an empty truck. It is not even true of most of them, for most of the men he sees on the street this weekday morning do, in fact, have jobs. But since, at the moment, they are neither working nor sleeping, and since they hate the depressing room or apartment they live in, or because there is nothing to do there,[2] or because they want to get away from their wives or anyone else living there, they are out on the street, indistinguishable from those who do not have jobs or do not want them. Some, like Boley, a member of a trash-collection crew in a suburban housing development, work Saturdays and are off on this weekday. Some, like Sweets, work nights cleaning up middle-class trash, dirt, dishes and garbage, and mopping the floors of the office buildings, hotels, restaurants, toilets and other public places dirtied during the day. Some men work for retail businesses such as liquor stores which do not begin the day until ten o'clock. Some laborers, like Tally, have already come back from the job because the ground was too wet for pick and shovel or because the weather was too cold for pouring concrete. Other employed men stayed off the job today for personal reasons: Clarence to go to a funeral at eleven this morning and Sea Cat to answer a subpoena as a witness in a criminal proceeding.

---

1. By different methods, perhaps, some social scientists have also located the problem in the men themselves, in their unwillingness or lack of desire to work: "To improve the underprivileged worker's performance, one must help him to learn to *want* . . . higher social goals for himself and his children. . . . The problem of changing the work habits and motivation of [lower class] people . . . is a problem of changing the goals, the ambitions, and the level of cultural and occupational aspiration of the underprivileged worker." (Emphasis in original.) Allison Davis, "The Motivation of the Underprivileged Worker," p. 90.

2. The comparison of sitting at home alone with being in jail is commonplace.

Also on the street, unwitting contributors to the impression taken away by the truck driver, are the halt and the lame. The man on the cast-iron steps strokes one gnarled arthritic hand with the other and says he doesn't know whether or not he'll live long enough to be eligible for Social Security. He pauses, then adds matter-of-factly, "Most times, I don't care whether I do or don't." Stoopy's left leg was polio-withered in childhood. Raymond, who looks as if he could tear out a fire hydrant, coughs up blood if he bends or moves suddenly. The quiet man who hangs out in front of the Saratoga apartments has a steel hook strapped onto his left elbow. And had the man in the truck been able to look into the wine-clouded eyes of the man in the green cap, he would have realized that the man did not even understand he was being offered a day's work.

Others, having had jobs and been laid off, are drawing unemployment compensation (up to $44 per week*) and have nothing to gain by accepting work which pays little more than this and frequently less.

Still others, like Bumdoodle the numbers man, are working hard at illegal ways of making money, hustlers who are on the street to turn a dollar any way they can: buying and selling sex, liquor, narcotics, stolen goods, or anything else that turns up.

Only a handful remains unaccounted for. There is Tonk, who cannot bring himself to take a job away from the corner, because, according to the other men, he suspects his wife will be unfaithful if given the opportunity. There is Stanton, who has not reported to work for four days now, not since Bernice disappeared. He bought a brand new knife against her return. She had done this twice before, he said, but not for so long and not without warning, and he had forgiven her. But this time, "I ain't got it in me to forgive her again." His rage and shame are there for all to see as

---

*U.S. Government Statistics indicate that $1.00 in 1967 (the year the first edition of *Tally's Corner* was published) is equivalent to about $5.50 in 2003. Rents in the District of Columbia are at least ten times greater in 2003 than they were in 1967.

he paces the Carry-out and the corner, day and night, hoping to catch a glimpse of her.

And finally, there are those like Arthur, able-bodied men who have no visible means of support, legal or illegal, who neither have jobs nor want them. The truck driver, among others, believes the Arthurs to be representative of all the men he sees idling on the street during his own working hours. They are not, but they cannot be dismissed simply because they are a small minority. It is not enough to explain them away as being lazy or irresponsible or both because an able-bodied man with responsibilities who refuses work is, by the truck driver's definition, lazy and irresponsible. Such an answer begs the question. It is descriptive of the facts; it does not explain them.

Moreover, despite their small numbers, the don't-work-and-don't-want-to-work minority is especially significant because they represent the strongest and clearest expression of those values and attitudes associated with making a living which, to varying degrees, are found throughout the streetcorner world. These men differ from the others in degree rather than in kind, the principal difference being that they are carrying out the implications of their values and experiences to their logical, inevitable conclusions. In this sense, the others have yet to come to terms with themselves and the world they live in.

Putting aside, for the moment, what the men say and feel, and looking at what they actually do and the choices they make, getting a job, keeping a job, and doing well at it is clearly of low priority. Arthur will not take a job at all. Leroy is supposed to be on his job at 4:00 p.m. but it is already 4:10 and he still cannot bring himself to leave the free games he has accumulated on the pinball machine in the Carry-out. Tonk started a construction job on Wednesday, worked Thursday and Friday, then didn't go back again. On the same kind of job, Sea Cat quit in the second week. Sweets had been working three months as a busboy in a restaurant, then quit without notice, not sure himself why he did so. A real estate agent, saying he was more interested in getting the job done than in the cost, asked Richard to give him an estimate on repairing and painting the inside of a house, but Richard, after looking over the job, somehow never got around to submitting an estimate. During one period, Tonk would not leave the corner to take a job because his wife might prove unfaithful; Stanton would not take a job because his woman had been unfaithful.

Thus, the man-job relationship is a tenuous one. At any given moment, a job may occupy a relatively low position on the streetcorner scale of real values. Getting a job may be subordinated to relations with women or to other non-job considerations; the commitment to a job one already has is frequently shallow and tentative.

The reasons are many. Some are objective and reside principally in the job; some are subjective and reside principally in the man. The line between them, however, is not a clear one. Behind the man's refusal to take a job or his decision to quit one is not a simple impulse or value choice but a complex combination of assessments of objective reality on the one hand, and values, attitudes and beliefs drawn from different levels of his experience on the other.

Objective economic considerations are frequently a controlling factor in a man's refusal to take a job. How much the job pays is a crucial question but seldom asked. He knows how much it pays. Working as a stock clerk, a delivery boy, or even behind the counter of liquor stores, drug stores and other retail businesses pays one dollar an hour. So, too, do most busboy, car-wash, janitorial and other jobs available to him. Some jobs, such as dishwasher, may dip as low as eighty cents an hour and others, such as elevator operator or work in a junk yard, may offer $1.15 or $1.25. Take-home pay for jobs such as these ranges from $35 to $50 a week, but a take-home pay of over $45 for a five-day week is the exception rather than the rule.

One of the principal advantages of these kinds of jobs is that they offer fairly regular work. Most of them involve essential services and are therefore somewhat less responsive to business conditions than are some higher paying, less menial jobs. Most of them are also inside jobs not dependent on the weather, as are construction jobs and other higher-paying outside work.

Another seemingly important advantage of working in hotels, restaurants, office and apartment buildings and retail establishments is that they frequently offer an opportunity for stealing on the job. But stealing can be a two-edged sword. Apart from increasing the cost of the goods or services to the general public, a less obvious result is that the practice usually acts as a depressant on the employee's own wage level. Owners of small retail establishments and other employers frequently anticipate employee stealing and adjust the wage rate accordingly. Tonk's employer explained why he was paying Tonk $35 for a 55–60 hour workweek. These men will all steal, he said. Although he keeps close watch on Tonk, he estimates that Tonk steals from $35 to $40 a week.[3] What he steals, when added to his regular earnings, brings his take-home pay to $70 or $75 per week. The employer said he did not mind this because Tonk is worth that much to the business. But if he were to pay Tonk outright the full value of his labor, Tonk would still be stealing $35–$40 per week and this, he said, the business simply would not support.

This wage arrangement, with stealing built-in, was satisfactory to both parties, with each one independently expressing his satisfaction. Such a wage-theft system, however, is not as balanced and equitable as it appears. Since the wage level rests on the premise that the employee will steal the unpaid value of his labor, the man who does not steal on the job is penalized. And furthermore, even if he does not steal, no one would believe him; the employer and others believe he steals because the system presumes it.

Nor is the man who steals, as he is expected to, as well off as he believes himself to be. The employer may occasionally close his

---

3. Exactly the same estimate as the one made by Tonk himself. On the basis of personal knowledge of the stealing routine employed by Tonk, however, I suspect the actual amount is considerably smaller.

eyes to the worker's stealing but not often and not for long. He is, after all, a businessman and cannot always find it within himself to let a man steal from him, even if the man is stealing his own wages. Moreover, it is only by keeping close watch on the worker that the employer can control how much is stolen and thereby protect himself against the employee's stealing more than he is worth. From this viewpoint, then, the employer is not in wage-theft collusion with the employee. In the case of Tonk, for instance, the employer was not actively abetting the theft. His estimate of how much Tonk was stealing was based on what he thought Tonk was able to steal despite his own best efforts to prevent him from stealing anything at all. Were he to have caught Tonk in the act of stealing, he would, of course, have fired him from the job and perhaps called the police as well. Thus, in an actual if not in a legal sense, all the elements of entrapment are present. The employer knowingly provides the conditions which entice (force) the employee to steal the unpaid value of his labor, but at the same time he punishes him for theft if he catches him doing so.

Other consequences of the wage-theft system are even more damaging to the employee. Let us, for argument's sake, say that Tonk is in no danger of entrapment; that his employer is willing to wink at the stealing and that Tonk, for his part, is perfectly willing to earn a little, steal a little. Let us say, too, that he is paid $35 a week and allowed to steal $35. His money income—as measured by the goods and services he can purchase with it—is, of course, $70. But not all of his income is available to him for all purposes. He cannot draw on what he steals to build his self-respect or to measure his self-worth. For this, he can draw only on his earnings—the amount given him publicly and voluntarily in exchange for his labor. His "respect" and "self-worth" income remains at $35—only half that of the man who also receives $70 but all of it in the form of wages. His earnings publicly measure the worth of his labor to his employer, and they are important to others and to himself in taking the measure of his worth as a man.[4]

---

4. Some public credit may accrue to the clever thief but not respect.

With or without stealing, and quite apart from any interior processes going on in the man who refuses such a job or quits it casually and without apparent reason, the objective fact is that menial jobs in retailing or in the service trades simply do not pay enough to support a man and his family. This is not to say that the worker is underpaid; this may or may not be true. Whether he is or not, the plain fact is that, in such a job, he cannot make a living. Nor can he take much comfort in the fact that these jobs tend to offer more regular, steadier work. If he cannot live on the $45 or $50 he makes in one week, the longer he works, the longer he cannot live on what he makes.[5]

Construction work, even for unskilled laborers, usually pays better, with the hourly rate ranging from $1.50 to $2.60 an hour.[6]

---

5. It might be profitable to compare, as Howard S. Becker suggests, gross aspects of income and housing costs in this particular area with those reported by Herbert Gans for the low-income working class in Boston's West End. In 1958, Gans reports, median income for the West Enders was just under $70 a week, a level considerably higher than that enjoyed by the people in the Carry-out neighborhood five years later. Gans himself rented a six-room apartment in the West End for $46 a month, about $10 more than the going rate for long-time residents. In the Carry-out neighborhood, rooms that could accommodate more than a cot and a miniature dresser— that is, rooms that qualified for family living—rented for $12 to $22 a week. Ignoring differences that really can't be ignored—the privacy and self-contained efficiency of the multi-room apartment as against the fragmented, public living of the rooming-house "apartment," with a public toilet on a floor always different from the one your room is on (no matter, it probably doesn't work, anyway)—and assuming comparable states of disrepair, the West Enders were paying $6 or $7 a month for a room that cost the Carry-outers at least $50 a month, and frequently more. Looking at housing costs as a percentage of income—and again ignoring what cannot be ignored: that what goes by the name of "housing" in the two areas is not at all the same thing—the median income West Ender could get a six-room apartment for about 12 percent of his income, while his 1963 Carry-out counterpart, with a weekly income of $60 (to choose a figure from the upper end of the income range), often paid 20–33 percent of his income for one room. See Herbert J. Gans, *The Urban Villagers*, pp. 10–13. [*Publisher's note:* For an update of the consumer price index to 2003, see http:// woodrow.mpls.frb.fed.us/research/data/us/calc/.]

6. The higher amount is 1962 union scale for building laborers. According to the Wage Agreement Contract for Heavy Construction Laborers (Washington, D.C.,

Importantly, too, good references, a good driving record, a tenth grade (or any high school) education, previous experience, the ability to "bring police clearance with you" are not normally required of laborers as they frequently are for some of the jobs in retailing or in the service trades.

Construction work, however, has its own objective disadvantages. It is, first of all, seasonal work for the great bulk of the laborers, beginning early in the spring and tapering off as winter weather sets in.[7] And even during the season the work is frequently irregular. Early or late in the season, snow or temperatures too low for concrete frequently sends the laborers back home, and during late spring or summer, a heavy rain on Tuesday or Wednesday, leaving a lot of water and mud behind it, can mean a two or three day work-week for the pick-and-shovel men and other unskilled laborers.[8]

The elements are not the only hazard. As the project moves from one construction stage to another, laborers—usually without

---

and vicinity) covering the period from May 1, 1963 to April 30, 1966, minimum hourly wage for heavy construction laborers was to go from $2.75 (May 1963) by annual increments to $2.92, effective November 1, 1965.

7. "Open-sky" work, such as building overpasses, highways, etc., in which the workers and materials are directly exposed to the elements, traditionally begins in March and ends around Thanksgiving. The same is true for much of the street repair work and the laying of sewer, electric, gas, and telephone lines by the city and public utilities, all important employers of laborers. Between Thanksgiving and March, they retain only skeleton crews selected from their best, most reliable men.

8. In a recent year, the crime rate in Washington for the month of August jumped 18 percent over the preceding month. A veteran police officer explained the increase to David L. Bazelon, Chief Judge, U.S. Court of Appeals for the District of Columbia. "It's quite simple. . . . You see, August was a very wet month. . . . These people wait on the street corner each morning around 6:00 or 6:30 for a truck to pick them up and take them to a construction site. If it's raining, that truck doesn't come, and the men are going to be idle that day. If the bad weather keeps up for three days . . . we know we are going to have trouble on our hands—and sure enough, there invariably follows a rash of purse-snatchings, house-breakings and the like. . . . These people have to eat like the rest of us, you know." David L. Bazelon, Address to the Federal Bar Association, p. 3.

warning—are laid off, sometimes permanently or sometimes for weeks at a time. The more fortunate or the better workers are told periodically to "take a walk for two, three days."

Both getting the construction job and getting to it are also relatively more difficult than is the case for the menial jobs in retailing and the service trades. Job competition is always fierce. In the city, the large construction projects are unionized. One has to have ready cash to get into the union to become eligible to work on these projects and, being eligible, one has to find an opening. Unless one "knows somebody," say a foreman or a laborer who knows the day before that they are going to take on new men in the morning, this can be a difficult and disheartening search.

Many of the nonunion jobs are in suburban Maryland or Virginia. The newspaper ads say, "Report ready to work to the trailer at the intersection of Rte. 11 and Old Bridge Rd., Bunston, Virginia (or Maryland)," but this location may be ten, fifteen, or even twenty-five miles from the Carry-out. Public transportation would require two or more hours to get there, if it services the area at all. Without access to a car or to a car-pool arrangement, it is not worthwhile reading the ad. So the men do not. Jobs such as these are usually filled by word of mouth information, beginning with someone who knows someone or who is himself working there and looking for a paying rider. Furthermore, nonunion jobs in outlying areas tend to be smaller projects of relatively short duration and to pay somewhat less than scale.

Still another objective factor is the work itself. For some men, whether the job be digging, mixing mortar, pushing a wheelbarrow, unloading materials, carrying and placing steel rods for reinforcing concrete, or building or laying concrete forms, the work is simply too hard. Men such as Tally and Wee Tom can make such work look like child's play; some of the older workhardened men, such as Budder and Stanton, can do it too, although not without showing unmistakable signs of strain and weariness at the end of the workday. But those who lack the robustness of a Tally or the time-inured immunity of a Budder must either forego jobs such as these or pay a heavy toll to keep them. For Leroy, in his early twenties, almost six feet tall but weighing under 140 pounds, it would be as difficult to push a loaded wheelbarrow, or to unload and stack 96-pound bags of cement all day long, as it would be for Stoopy with his withered leg.

Heavy, backbreaking labor of the kind that used to be regularly associated with bull gangs or concrete gangs is no longer characteristic of laboring jobs, especially those with the larger, well-equipped construction companies. Brute strength is still required from time to time, as on smaller jobs where it is not economical to bring in heavy equipment or where the small, undercapitalized contractor has none to bring in. In many cases, however, the conveyor belt has replaced the wheelbarrow or the Georgia buggy, mechanized forklifts have eliminated heavy, manual lifting, and a variety of digging machines have replaced the pick and shovel. The result is fewer jobs for unskilled laborers and, in many cases, a work speed-up for those who do have jobs. Machines now set the pace formerly set by men. Formerly, a laborer pushed a wheelbarrow of wet cement to a particular spot, dumped it, and returned for another load. Another laborer, in hip boots, pushed the wet concrete around with a shovel or a hoe, getting it roughly level in preparation for the skilled finishers. He had relatively small loads to contend with and had only to keep up with the men pushing the wheelbarrows. Now, the job for the man pushing the wheelbarrow is gone and the wet concrete comes rushing down a chute at the man in the hip boots who must "spread it quick or drown."

Men who have been running an elevator, washing dishes, or "pulling trash" cannot easily move into laboring jobs. They lack the basic skills for "unskilled" construction labor, familiarity with tools and materials, and tricks of the trade without which hard jobs are made harder. Previously unused or untrained muscles rebel in pain against the new and insistent demands made upon them, seriously compromising the man's performance and testing his willingness to see the job through.

A healthy, sturdy, active man of good intelligence requires from two to four weeks to break in on a construction job.[9] Even if he is willing somehow to bull his way through the first few weeks, it frequently happens that his foreman or the craftsman he services with materials and general assistance is not willing to wait that long for him to get into condition or to learn at a glance the difference in size between a rough 2″ × 8″ and a finished 2″ × 10″. The foreman and the craftsman are themselves "under the gun" and cannot "carry" the man when other men, who are already used to the work and who know the tools and materials, are lined up to take the job.

Sea Cat was "healthy, sturdy, active and of good intelligence." When a judge gave him six weeks in which to pay his wife $200 in back child-support payments, he left his grocery-store job in order to take a higher-paying job as a laborer, arranged for him by a foreman friend. During the first week the weather was bad and he worked only Wednesday and Friday, cursing the elements all the while for cheating him out of the money he could have made. The second week, the weather was fair but he quit at the end of the fourth day, saying frankly that the work was too hard for him. He went back to his job at the grocery store and took a second job working nights as a dishwasher in a restaurant,[10] earning little if any more at the two jobs than he would have earned as a laborer, and keeping at both of them until he had paid off his debts.

Tonk did not last as long as Sea Cat. No one made any predictions when he got a job in a parking lot, but when the men on the corner learned he was to start on a road construction job, estimates of how long he would last ranged from one to three weeks. Wednesday was his first day. He spent that evening and night at home. He did the same on Thursday. He worked Friday and spent

---

9. Estimate of Mr. Francis Greenfield, President of the International Hod Carriers, Euilding and Common Laborers' District Council of Washington, D.C. and Vicinity. I am indebted to Mr. Greenfield for several points in these paragraphs dealing with construction laborers.

10. Not a sinecure, even by streetcorner standards.

Friday evening and part of Saturday draped over the mailbox on the corner. Sunday afternoon, Tonk decided he was not going to report on the job the next morning. He explained that after working three days, he knew enough about the job to know that it was too hard for him. He knew he wouldn't be able to keep up and he'd just as soon quit now as get fired later.

Logan was a tall, two-hundred-pound man in his late twenties. His back used to hurt him only on the job, he said, but now he can't straighten up for increasingly longer periods of time. He said he had traced this to the awkward walk he was forced to adopt by the loaded wheelbarrows which pull him down into a half-stoop. He's going to quit, he said, as soon as he can find another job. If he can't find one real soon, he guesses he'll quit anyway. It's not worth it, having to walk bent over and leaning to one side.

Sometimes, the strain and effort is greater than the man is willing to admit, even to himself. In the early summer of 1963, Richard was rooming at Nancy's place. His wife and children were "in the country" (his grandmother's home in Carolina), waiting for him to save up enough money so that he could bring them back to Washington and start over again after a disastrous attempt to "make it" in Philadelphia. Richard had gotten a job with a fence company in Virginia. It paid $1.60 an hour. The first few evenings, when he came home from work, he looked ill from exhaustion and the heat. Stanton said Richard would have to quit, "he's too small [thin] for that kind of work." Richard said he was doing O.K. and would stick with the job.

At Nancy's one night, when Richard had been working about two weeks, Nancy and three or four others were sitting around talking, drinking, and listening to music. Someone asked Nancy when was Richard going to bring his wife and children up from the country. Nancy said she didn't know, but it probably depended on how long it would take him to save up enough money. She said she didn't think he could stay with the fence job much longer. This morning, she said, the man Richard rode to work with knocked on the door and Richard didn't answer. She looked in his room. Richard was still asleep. Nancy tried to shake him awake. "No more digging!" Richard cried out. "No more digging! I can't do no more God-damn digging!" When Nancy finally managed to wake him, he dressed quickly and went to work.

Richard stayed on the job two more weeks, then suddenly quit, ostensibly because his pay check was three dollars less than what he thought it should have been.

In summary of objective job considerations, then, the most important fact is that a man who is able and willing to work cannot earn enough money to support himself, his wife, and one or more children. A man's chances for working regularly are good only if he is willing to work for less than he can live on, and sometimes not even then. On some jobs, the wage rate is deceptively higher than on others, but the higher the wage rate, the more difficult it is to get the job, and the less the job security. Higher-paying construction work tends to be seasonal and, during the season, the amount of work available is highly sensitive to business and weather conditions and to the changing requirements of individual projects.[11] Moreover, high-paying construction jobs are frequently beyond the physical capacity of some of the men, and some of the low-paying jobs are scaled down even lower in accordance with the self-fulfilling assumption that the man will steal part of his wages on the job.[12]

---

11. The overall result is that, in the long run, a Negro laborer's earnings are not substantially greater—and may be less—than those of the busboy, janitor, or stock clerk. Herman P. Miller, for example, reports that in 1960, 40 percent of all jobs held by Negro men were as laborers or in the service trades. The average annual wage for nonwhite nonfarm laborers was $2,400. The average earning of nonwhite service workers was $2,500 (*Rich Man, Poor Man*, p. 90). Francis Greenfield estimates that in the Washington vicinity, the 1965 earnings of the union laborer who works whenever work is available will be about $3,200. Even this figure is high for the man on the streetcorner. Union men in heavy construction are the aristocrats of the laborers. Casual day labor and jobs with small firms in the building and construction trades, or with firms in other industries, pay considerably less.

12. For an excellent discussion of the self-fulfilling assumption (or prophecy) as a social force, see "The Self-Fulfilling Prophecy," Ch. XI, in Robert K. Merton's *Social Theory and Social Structure*.

Bernard assesses the objective job situation dispassionately over a cup of coffee, sometimes poking at the coffee with his spoon, sometimes staring at it as if, like a crystal ball, it holds tomorrow's secrets. He is twenty-seven years old. He and the woman with whom he lives have a baby son, and she has another child by another man. Bernard does odd jobs—mostly painting—but here it is the end of January, and his last job was with the Post Office during the Christmas mail rush. He would like postal work as a steady job, he says. It pays well (about $2.00 an hour) but he has twice failed the Post Office examination (he graduated from a Washington high school) and has given up the idea as an impractical one. He is supposed to see a man tonight about a job as a parking attendant for a large apartment house. The man told him to bring his birth certificate and driver's license, but his license was suspended because of a backlog of unpaid traffic fines. A friend promised to lend him some money this evening. If he gets it, he will pay the fines tomorrow morning and have his license reinstated. He hopes the man with the job will wait till tomorrow night.

A "security job" is what he really wants, he said. He would like to save up money for a taxicab. (But having twice failed the postal examination and having a bad driving record as well, it is highly doubtful that he could meet the qualifications or pass the written test.) That would be "a good life." He can always get a job in a restaurant or as a clerk in a drugstore but they don't pay enough, he said. He needs to take home at least $50 to $55 a week. He thinks he can get that much driving a truck somewhere . . . Sometimes he wishes he had stayed in the army . . . A security job, that's what he wants most of all, a real security job . . .

When we look at what the men bring to the job rather than at what the job offers the men, it is essential to keep in mind that we are not looking at men who come to the job fresh, just out of school perhaps, and newly prepared to undertake the task of making a living, or from another job where they earned a living and are prepared to do the same on this job. Each man comes to the job with a long job history characterized by his not being able to support himself and his family. Each man carries this knowledge, born of his experience, with him. He comes to the job flat and stale, wearied by the sameness of it all, convinced of his own incompetence, terrified of responsibility—of being tested still again and found wanting. Possible exceptions are the younger men not yet, or just, married. They suspect all this but have yet to have it confirmed by repeated personal experience over time. But those who are or have been married know it well. It is the experience of the individual and the group; of their fathers and probably their sons. Convinced of their inadequacies, not only do they not seek out those few better-paying jobs which test their resources, but they actively avoid them, gravitating in a mass to the menial, routine jobs which offer no challenge—and therefore pose no threat—to the already diminished images they have of themselves.

Thus Richard does not follow through on the real estate agent's offer. He is afraid to do on his own—minor plastering, replacing broken windows, other minor repairs and painting—exactly what he had been doing for months on a piecework basis under someone else (and which provided him with a solid base from which to derive a cost estimate). Richard once offered an important clue to what may have gone on in his mind when the job offer was made. We were in the Carry-out, at a time when he was looking for work. He was talking about the kind of jobs available to him.

> I graduated from high school [Baltimore] but I don't know anything. I'm dumb. Most of the time I don't even say I graduated, 'cause then somebody asks me a question and I can't answer it, and they think I was lying about graduating. . . . They graduated me but I didn't know anything. I had lousy grades but I guess they wanted to get rid of me.
>
> I was at Margaret's house the other night and her little sister asked me to help her with her homework. She showed me some fractions and I knew right away I couldn't do them. I was ashamed so I told her I had to go to the bathroom.

And so it must have been, surely, with the real estate agent's offer. Convinced that "I'm dumb . . . I don't know anything," he "knew right away" he couldn't do it, despite the fact that he had been doing just this sort of work all along.

Thus, the man's low self-esteem generates a fear of being tested and prevents him from accepting a job with responsibilities or, once on a job, from staying with it if responsibilities are thrust on him, even if the wages are commensurately higher. Richard refuses such a job, Leroy leaves one, and another man, given more responsibility and more pay, knows he will fail and proceeds to do so, proving he was right about himself all along. The self-fulfilling prophecy is everywhere at work. In a hallway, Stanton, Tonk and Boley are passing a bottle around. Stanton recalls the time he was in the service. Everything was fine until he attained the rank of corporal. He worried about everything he did then. Was he doing the right thing? Was he doing it well? When would they discover their mistake and take his stripes (and extra pay) away? When he finally lost his stripes, everything was all right again.

Lethargy, disinterest and general apathy on the job, so often reported by employers, has its streetcorner counterpart. The men do not ordinarily talk about their jobs or ask one another about them.[13] Although most of the men know who is or is not working at any given time, they may or may not know what particular job an individual man has. There is no overt interest in job specifics as they relate to this or that person, in large part perhaps because the specifics are not especially relevant. To know that a man is working is to know approximately how much he makes and to know as much as one needs or wants to know about how he makes it.

---

13. This stands in dramatic contrast to the leisure-time conversation of stable, working-class men. For the coal miners (of Ashton, England), for example, "the topic [of conversation] which surpasses all others in frequency is work—the difficulties which have been encountered in the day's shift, the way in which a particular task was accomplished, and so on." Josephine Klein, *Samples from English Cultures*, Vol. I, p. 88.

After all, how much difference does it make to know whether a man is pushing a mop and pulling trash in an apartment house, a restaurant, or an office building, or delivering groceries, drugs, or liquor, or, if he's a laborer, whether he's pushing a wheelbarrow, mixing mortar, or digging a hole. So much does one job look like every other that there is little to choose between them. In large part, the job market consists of a narrow range of nondescript chores calling for nondistinctive, undifferentiated, unskilled labor. "A job is a job."

A crucial factor in the streetcorner man's lack of job commitment is the overall value he places on the job. *For his part, the streetcorner man puts no lower value on the job than does the larger society around him.* He knows the social value of the job by the amount of money the employer is willing to pay him for doing it. In a real sense, every pay day, he counts in dollars and cents the value placed on the job by society at large. He is no more (and frequently less) ready to quit and look for another job than his employer is ready to fire him and look for another man. Neither the streetcorner man who performs these jobs nor the society which requires him to perform them assesses the job as one "worth doing and worth doing well." Both employee and employer are contemptuous of the job. The employee shows his contempt by his reluctance to accept it or keep it, the employer by paying less than is required to support a family.[14] Nor does the low-wage job offer prestige, respect, interesting work, opportunity for learning or advancement, or any other compensation. With few exceptions, jobs filled by the streetcorner men are at the bottom of the employment ladder in every respect, from wage level to prestige. Typically, they are hard, dirty, uninteresting and underpaid. The rest of

---

14. It is important to remember that the employer is not entirely a free agent. Subject to the constraints of the larger society, he acts for the larger society as well as for himself. Child labor laws, safety and sanitation regulations, minimum wage scales in some employment areas, and other constraints, are already on the books; other control mechanisms, such as a guaranteed annual wage, are to be had for the voting.

society (whatever its ideal values regarding the dignity of labor) holds the job of the dishwasher or janitor or unskilled laborer in low esteem if not outright contempt.[15] So does the streetcorner man. He cannot do otherwise. He cannot draw from a job those social values which other people do not put into it.[16]

Only occasionally does spontaneous conversation touch on these matters directly. Talk about jobs is usually limited to isolated statements of intention, such as "I think I'll get me another gig [job]," "I'm going to look for a construction job when the weather breaks," or "I'm going to quit. I can't take no more of his shit." Job assessments typically consist of nothing more than a noncommittal shrug and "It's O.K." or "It's a job."

One reason for the relative absence of talk about one's job is, as suggested earlier, that the sameness of job experiences does not bear reiteration. Another and more important reason is the emptiness of the job experience itself. The man sees middle-class occupations as a primary source of prestige, pride and self-respect; his own job affords him none of these. To think about his job is to see himself as others see him, to remind him of just where he stands in this society.[17] And because society's criteria for placement are

---

15. See, for example, the U.S. Bureau of the Census, *Methodology and Scores of Socioeconomic Status*. The assignment of the lowest SES ratings to men who hold such jobs is not peculiar to our own society. A low SES rating for "the shoeshine boy or garbage man . . . seems to be true for all [industrial] countries." Alex Inkeles, "Industrial Man," p. 8.

16. That the streetcorner man downgrades manual labor should occasion no surprise. Merton points out that "the American stigmatization of manual labor . . . *has been found to hold rather uniformly in all social classes*" (emphasis in original; *Social Theory and Social Structure*, p. 145). That he finds no satisfaction in such work should also occasion no surprise: "[There is] a clear positive correlation between the over-all status of occupations and the experience of satisfaction in them." Inkeles, "Industrial Man," p. 12.

17. "[In our society] a man's work is one of the things by which he is judged, and certainly one of the more significant things by which he judges himself. . . . A man's work is one of the more important parts of his social identity, of his self; indeed, of his fate in the one life he has to live." Everett C. Hughes, *Men and Their Work*, pp. 42–43.

generally the same as his own, to talk about his job can trigger a flush of shame and a deep, almost physical ache to change places with someone, almost anyone, else.[18] The desire to be a person in his own right, to be noticed by the world he lives in, is shared by each of the men on the streetcorner. Whether they articulate this desire (as Tally does below) or not, one can see them position themselves to catch the attention of their fellows in much the same way as plants bend or stretch to catch the sunlight.[19]

Tally and I were in the Carry-out. It was summer, Tally's peak earning season as a cement finisher, a semiskilled job a cut or so above that of the unskilled laborer. His take-home pay during these weeks was well over a hundred dollars—"a lot of bread." But for Tally, who no longer had a family to support, bread was not enough.

> "You know that boy came in last night? That Black Moozlem? That's what I ought to be doing, ought to be in his place."
>
> "What do you mean?"
>
> "Dressed nice, going to [night] school, got a good job."
>
> "He's no better off than you, Tally. You make more than he does."
>
> "It's not the money. [Pause] It's position, I guess. He's got position. When he finish school he gonna be a supervisor. People respect him. . . . Thinking about people with position and education gives me a feeling right here [pressing his fingers into the pit of his stomach]."

---

18. Noting that lower-class persons "are constantly exposed to evidence of their own irrelevance," Lee Rainwater spells out still another way in which the poor are poor: "The identity problems of lower class persons make the soul-searching of middle class adolescents and adults seem rather like a kind of conspicuous consumption of psychic riches" ("Work and Identity in the Lower Class," p. 3).

19. Sea Cat cuts his pants legs off at the calf and puts a fringe on the raggedy edges. Tonk breaks his "shades" and continues to wear the horn-rimmed frames minus the lenses. Richard cultivates a distinctive manner of speech. Lonny gives himself a birthday party. And so on.

"You're educated, too. You have a skill, a trade. You're a cement finisher. You can make a building, pour a sidewalk."

"That's different. Look, can anybody do what you're doing?
Can anybody just come up and do your job? Well, in one week I
can teach you cement finishing. You won't be as good as me 'cause
you won't have the experience but you'll be a cement finisher.
That's what I mean. Anybody can do what I'm doing and that's
what gives me this feeling. [Long pause] Suppose I like this girl. I
go over to her house and I meet her father. He starts talking about
what he done today. He talks about operating on somebody and
sewing them up and about surgery. I know he's a doctor 'cause of
the way he talks. Then she starts talking about what she did. Maybe
she's a boss or a supervisor. Maybe she's a lawyer and her father says
to me, 'And what do you do, Mr. Jackson?' [Pause] You remember
at the courthouse, Lonny's trial? You and the lawyer was talking in
the hall? You remember? I just stood there listening. I didn't say a
word. You know why? 'Cause I didn't even know what you was
talking about. That's happened to me a lot."

"Hell, you're nothing special. That happens to everybody. Nobody knows everything. One man is a doctor, so he talks about
surgery. Another man is a teacher, so he talks about books. But doc-
tors and teachers don't know anything about concrete. You're a cement finisher and that's your specialty."

"Maybe so, but when was the last time you saw anybody
standing around talking about concrete?"

The streetcorner man wants to be a person in his own right,
to be noticed, to be taken of, but in this respect, as well as in meeting his money needs, his job fails him. The job and the man are
even. The job fails the man and the man fails the job.

Furthermore, the man does not have any reasonable expecta-
tion that, however bad it is, his job will lead to better things. Menial jobs are not, by and large, the starting point of a track system
which leads to even better jobs for those who are able and willing
to do them. The busboy or dishwasher in a restaurant is not on a

job track which, if negotiated skillfully, leads to chef or manager of the restaurant. The busboy or dishwasher who works hard becomes, simply, a hard-working busboy or dishwasher. Neither hard work nor perseverance can conceivably carry the janitor to a sit-down job in the office building he cleans up. And it is the apprentice who becomes the journeyman electrician, plumber, steam fitter or bricklayer, not the common unskilled Negro laborer.

Thus, the job is not a stepping stone to something better. It is a dead end. It promises to deliver no more tomorrow, next month or next year than it does today.

Delivering little, and promising no more, the job is "no big thing." The man appears to treat the job in a cavalier fashion, working and not working as the spirit moves him, as if all that matters is the immediate satisfaction of his present appetites, the surrender to present moods, and the indulgence of whims with no thought for the cost, the consequences, the future. To the middle-class observer, this behavior reflects a "present-time orientation"—an "inability to defer gratification." It is this "present-time" orientation—as against the "future orientation" of the middle-class person—that "explains" to the outsider why Leroy chooses to spend the day at the Carry-out rather than report to work; why Richard, who was paid Friday, was drunk Saturday and Sunday and penniless Monday; why Sweets quit his job today because the boss looked at him "funny" yesterday.

But from the inside looking out, what appears as a "present-time" orientation to the outside observer is, to the man experiencing it, as much a future orientation as that of his middle-class counterpart.[20] The difference between the two men lies not so much in their different orientations to time as in their different orientations to future time or, more specifically, to their different futures.[21]

---

20. Taking a somewhat different point of view, S. M. Miller and Frank Riessman suggest that "the entire concept of deferred gratification may be inappropriate to understanding the essence of workers' lives" ("The Working Class Subculture: A New View," p. 87).

21. This sentence is a paraphrase of a statement made by Marvin Cline at a 1965 colloquium at the Mental Health Study Center, National Institute of Mental Health.

The future orientation of the middle-class person presumes, among other things, a surplus of resources to be invested in the future and a belief that the future will be sufficiently stable both to justify his investment (money in a bank, time and effort in a job, investment of himself in marriage and family, etc.) and to permit the consumption of his investment at a time, place and manner of his own choosing and to his greater satisfaction. But the street-corner man lives in a sea of want. He does not, as a rule, have a surplus of resources, either economic or psychological. Gratification of hunger and the desire for simple creature comforts cannot be long deferred. Neither can support for one's flagging self-esteem. Living on the edge of both economic and psychological subsistence, the streetcorner man is obliged to expend all his resources on maintaining himself from moment to moment.[22]

As for the future, the young streetcorner man has a fairly good picture of it. In Richard or Sea Cat or Arthur he can see himself in his middle twenties; he can look at Tally to see himself at thirty, at Wee Tom to see himself in his middle thirties, and at Budder and Stanton to see himself in his forties. It is a future in which everything is uncertain except the ultimate destruction of his hopes and the eventual realization of his fears. The most he can reasonably look forward to is that these things do not come too

22. And if, for the moment, he does sometimes have more money than he chooses to spend or more food than he wants to eat, he is pressed to spend the money and eat the food anyway since his friends, neighbors, kinsmen, or acquaintances will beg or borrow whatever surplus he has or, failing this, they may steal it. In one extreme case, one of the men admitted taking the last of a woman's surplus food allotment after she had explained that, with four children, she could not spare any food. The prospect that consumer soft goods not consumed by oneself will be consumed by someone else may be related to the way in which portable consumer durable goods, such as watches, radios, television sets or phonographs, are sometimes looked at as a form of savings. When Shirley was on welfare, she regularly took her television set out of pawn when she got her monthly check. Not so much to watch it, she explained, as to have something to fall back on when her money runs out toward the end of the month. For her and others, the television set or the phonograph is her savings, the pawnshop is where she banks her savings, and the pawn ticket is her bankbook.

soon. Thus, when Richard squanders a week's pay in two days it is not because, like an animal or a child, he is "present-time oriented," unaware of or unconcerned with his future. He does so precisely because he is aware of the future and the hopelessness of it all.

Sometimes this kind of response appears as a conscious, explicit choice. Richard had had a violent argument with his wife. He said he was going to leave her and the children, that he had had enough of everything and could not take any more, and he chased her out of the house. His chest still heaving, he leaned back against the wall in the hallway of his basement apartment.

> "I've been scuffling for five years," he said. "I've been scuffling for five years from morning till night. And my kids still don't have anything, my wife don't have anything, and I don't have anything.
>
> "There," he said, gesturing down the hall to a bed, a sofa, a couple of chairs and a television set, all shabby, some broken. "There's everything I have and I'm having trouble holding onto that."
>
> Leroy came in, presumably to petition Richard on behalf of Richard's wife, who was sitting outside on the steps, afraid to come in. Leroy started to say something but Richard cut him short.
>
> "Look, Leroy, don't give me any of that action. You and me are entirely different people. Maybe I look like a boy and maybe I act like a boy sometimes but I got a man's mind. You and me don't want the same things out of life. Maybe some of the same, but you don't care how long you have to wait for yours and I—*want—mine—right—now.*"[23]

---

23. This was no simple rationalization for irresponsibility. Richard had indeed "been scuffling for five years" trying to keep his family going. Until shortly after this episode, Richard was known and respected as one of the hardest-working men on the street. Richard had said, only a couple of months earlier, "I figure you got to get out there and try. You got to try before you can get anything." His wife Shirley confirmed that he had always tried. "If things get tough, with me I'll get all worried. But Richard get worried, he don't want me to see him worried. . . . He *will* get out

Thus, apparent present-time concerns with consumption and indulgences—material and emotional—reflect a future-time orientation. "I want mine right now" is ultimately a cry of despair, a direct response to the future as he sees it.[24]

In many instances, it is precisely the streetcorner man's orientation to the future—but to a future loaded with "trouble"—which not only leads to a greater emphasis on present concerns ("I want mine right now") but also contributes importantly to the instability of employment, family and friend relationships, and to the general transient quality of daily life.

Let me give some concrete examples. One day, after Tally had gotten paid, he gave me four twenty-dollar bills and asked me to keep them for him. Three days later he asked me for the money. I returned it and asked why he did not put his money in a bank. He said that the banks close at two o'clock. I argued that there were four or more banks within a two-block radius of where he was

---

there. He's shoveled snow, picked beans, and he's done some of everything. . . . He's not ashamed to get out there and get us something to eat." At the time of the episode reported above, Leroy was just starting marriage and raising a family. He and Richard were not, as Richard thought, "entirely different people." Leroy had just not learned, by personal experience over time, what Richard had learned. But within two years Leroy's marriage had broken up and he was talking and acting like Richard. "He just let go completely," said one of the men on the street.

24. There is no mystically intrinsic connection between "present-time" orientation and lower-class persons. Whenever people of whatever class have been uncertain, skeptical or downright pessimistic about the future, "I want mine right now" has been one of the characteristic responses, although it is usually couched in more delicate terms: e.g., Omar Khayyam's "Take the cash and let the credit go," or Horace's "*Carpe diem.*" In wartime, especially, all classes tend to slough off conventional restraints on sexual and other behavior (i.e., become less able or less willing to defer gratification). And when inflation threatens, darkening the fiscal future, persons who formerly husbanded their resources with commendable restraint almost stampede one another rushing to spend their money. Similarly, it seems that future-time orientation tends to collapse toward the present when persons are in pain or under stress. The point here is that the label notwithstanding, (what passes for) present-time orientation appears to be a situation-specific phenomenon rather than a part of the standard psychic equipment of Cognitive Lower Class Man.

working at the time and that he could easily get to any one of them on his lunch hour. "No, man," he said, "you don't understand. They close at two o'clock and they closed Saturday and Sunday. Suppose I get into trouble and I got to make it [leave]. Me get out of town, and everything I got in the world layin' up in that bank? No good! No good!"

In another instance, Leroy and his girl friend were discussing "trouble." Leroy was trying to decide how best to go about getting his hands on some "long green" (a lot of money), and his girl friend cautioned him about "trouble." Leroy sneered at this, saying he had had "trouble" all his life and wasn't afraid of a little more. "Anyway," he said, "I'm famous for leaving town."[25]

Thus, the constant awareness of a future loaded with "trouble" results in a constant readiness to leave, to "make it," to "get out of town," and discourages the man from sinking roots into the world he lives in.[26] Just as it discourages him from putting money in the bank, so it discourages him from committing himself to a job, especially one whose payoff lies in the promise of future rewards rather than in the present. In the same way, it discourages him from deep and lasting commitments to family and friends or to any other persons, places or things, since such commitments could hold him hostage, limiting his freedom of movement and thereby compromising his security which lies in that freedom.

What lies behind the response to the driver of the pickup truck, then, is a complex combination of attitudes and assessments. The streetcorner man is under continuous assault by his job experiences and job fears. His experiences and fears feed on one another. The kind of job he can get—and frequently only after

---

25. And proceeded to do just that the following year when "trouble"—in this case, a grand jury indictment, a pile of debts, and a violent separation from his wife and children—appeared again.

26. For a discussion of "trouble" as a focal concern of lower-class culture, see Walter Miller, "Lower Class Culture as a Generating Milieu of Gang Delinquency," pp. 7, 8.

fighting for it, if then—steadily confirms his fears, depresses his self-confidence and self-esteem until finally, terrified of an opportunity even if one presents itself, he stands defeated by his experiences, his belief in his own self-worth destroyed and his fears a confirmed reality.

3

FATHERS WITHOUT CHILDREN

In the springtime, on a Sunday afternoon, Richard's four-year-old son lay seriously ill in Ward E of Children's Hospital. He and the other twelve children in the ward, almost all from low-income Negro families, were being visited by some twenty-five relatives and friends. Not a single man was among the visitors.

The men had their reasons. Some had separated from their wives and children and did not know their children were hospitalized. Others knew but couldn't or wouldn't make it. Richard had intended going but something came up, he would probably go tomorrow, and anyway, he never did like being in a hospital, not even to visit someone else.

But whether the fathers were living with their children or not, the result was the same: there were no men visiting the children in Ward E. This absence of the father is one of the chief characteristics of the father-child relationship.

The father-child relationship, however, is not the same for all streetcorner fathers, nor does a given relationship necessarily remain constant over time. Some fathers are not always "absent" and some are less "absent" than others. Moreover, the same father may have relationships of different intensity with his different children at the same time. The spectrum of father-child relationships is a

broad one, ranging from complete ignorance of the child's existence to continuous, day-by-day contact between father and child.
The emotional content of the relationships ranges from what, to
the outside observer, may seem on the father's part callous indiffer-
ence or worse, all the way to hinted private intimacies whose intensity can only be guessed at.

Leaving aside, for the present, the emotional and affective
content, father-child relationships can be grossly sorted out and located along a spectrum based upon the father's willingness to acknowledge paternity, his willingness to acknowledge responsibility
for and to provide financial support, and the frequency and duration of contact. At the low end of the spectrum are those relationships in which the children are born of casual, short-term, even
single-encounter unions; at the high end are legitimate children of
married parents, all of whom live in the same household. Since the
majority of streetcorner men do not live in the same households
as their children, the majority of father-child relationships appear
at the low and low-middle bands of the spectrum. The number
falls off quickly as one approaches the other end.

At the low end of the spectrum there may be no father-child
relationship at all. In some cases, the father may not know he is
the father of the child; in others, even the mother may not know
who the father is. Here, too, at the low end, are those fathers who
acknowledge possible or actual paternity but who have had no
subsequent contact with mother or child. Such seems to be the
case with many of the men who, while still in their teens, had a
baby "back home." Thus, Richard recalls that, before his marriage
to Shirley, a girl told him he was the father of her child. He did
nothing about it and neither did she "because there was nothing
she could do."[1] Richard subsequently saw the mother and child
on the street during a visit back home but did not speak to them.

---

1. He explained that "back home" a (Negro) woman in such a predicament has
no legal recourse. It she files a paternity suit, the judge asks her if the putative father
forced himself on her. When she admits he did not, the judge dismisses the case.

His sheepish laugh seemed a mixture of masculine pride and guilty embarrassment as he admitted that the child looked startlingly like himself.

Somewhat further along the spectrum are the relationships of Wesley and Earl with their children. Each has a child "back home" in the Carolinas and each acknowledges his paternity. Wesley has visited his hometown and has seen the mother of his child once or twice since the birth of the baby. Wesley and the child's mother are on friendly terms but Wesley gives her nothing and she asks for nothing. Earl's child also lives with its mother but Earl and the mother have remained fond of one another. Earl sees her regularly and sometimes sees the child, too, on those two or three times a year he goes back home. If he has spare cash, he leaves it with her for the baby.

In the middle range of the spectrum are the father-child relationships of those once-married men who, though separated from their wives and children, remain accessible to them. These men admit to a financial responsibility for their children, provide emergency and sometimes routine financial support, and are more or less informed about their children's general well-being. Contacts between the men and their separated families are almost always initiated by the mothers, usually for the purpose of getting money for the children. Sea Cat's wife calls him on the telephone in his rooming house to tell him when she is coming. Sometimes she brings one or both of their children, sometimes not. Stoopy's wife does not usually call. She comes on Saturday mornings, brings the two children along and stays for an hour or two.

Relationships in this middle range are by no means limited to legitimate children. Tally is the father of Bess's eighteen-month-old son. For a time, at least, their relationship was indistinguishable from Sea Cat's and Stoopy's relationships with their wives and children. On Tally's pay day, Bess would sometimes call the Carryout shop and ask that Tally be told she would be there that evening. Tally would meet her on the corner, pay her taxicab fare, then give her five or ten dollars for a doctor, a pair of shoes, or other extra expenses for the child.

In those few cases where the child is cared for by the father's mother or other members of his family, the father-child relationship seems to be closer than when the child is with the mother or member of her family. Such a child regularly carries the father's family name. The father provides at least partial financial support. He is often informed of the child's special needs and general well-being and, even where they are separated by great distances, father and child see each other one or more times during the year. Sweets, for example, has a child "back home." The child is being raised by Sweets's mother. Occasional letters are exchanged during the course of the year, and there are birthday cards and gifts for the child. Sweets manages to get down there for one or two weekends a year and, during the summer, his mother and his child come to spend a week or two with him in Washington. Tonk's relationship with his seven-year-old daughter, also "back home" where she is raised by Tonk's mother, is an even stronger one. They exchange letters and gifts and, at school's end, she comes to spend the whole summer with him. Stanton's daughter lives with his "sister"[2] only two blocks from where Stanton lives. The daughter remains his financial responsibility and, depending on circumstance or need, she moves in with him occasionally for short periods of time.

At the high end of the spectrum are those relationships where father and child are regular members of the same household. In such cases, even when the father and mother are not formally married to one another, there is no question but that the child carries the father's family name. Whether his wife is working or not, and unlike the men who are separated from their children, the father who is living with his children is, in his own eyes and in the eyes of those around him, charged with the day-to-day support of his

---

2. Stanton and this (unrelated) woman "go for brother and sister." See pp. 112–113.

wife and children. Father and child, as members of the same household, are in more or less continuous contact.

Looking at the spectrum as a whole, the modal father-child relationship for these streetcorner men seems to be one in which the father is separated from the child, acknowledges his paternity, admits to financial responsibility but provides financial support irregularly, if at all, and then only on demand or request. His contacts with the child are infrequent, irregular, and of short (minutes or hours) duration.

When we look away from these more formal aspects of father-child relationships and turn to their quality and texture, a seeming paradox emerges. The men who do not live with their own children seem to express more affection for their children and treat them more tenderly than those who do live with them. Moreover, the men are frequently more affectionate toward other men's children than toward their own.

Fathers who live with their children, for example, seem to take no pleasure in their children and give them little of their time and attention. They seldom mention their children in casual conversation and are never seen sitting or playing with them on the steps or in the street. The fathers do not take their children to tag along while they lounge on the streetcorner or in the Carry-out, nor do they, as they see other fathers in the neighborhood do, promenade with them on Easter Sunday or take them for walks on any other Sunday or holiday. When the father walks into the home, the child may not even look up from what he is doing and the father, for his part, takes no more notice than he receives. If their eyes happen to catch one another's glances, father and child seem to look without seeing until one or the other looks elsewhere.

Perhaps this routine absence of warmth and affection accounts for the way in which an offhand gesture by the father can suddenly deepen the relationship for the child, for however brief a time. John casually distributed some change among his six children. His wife Lorena describes what happened:

He give Buddy and the others a dime. You'd think Jesus had laid
something on them. They went all around the neighborhood brag-
ging their daddy give them a dime. I give them nickels and dimes
all day long and they don't think anything about it. But John, he
can give them a dime and they act like he gave them the whole
world.

Since father and child are seldom together outside the home,
it is in the home that casual gestures bespeaking paternal warmth
and tenderness are most likely to occur. Leroy and two friends are
in Leroy's house passing the time. Leroy sits on the bed and ab-
sentmindedly strokes the head of his small son lying next to him.
In Richard's house, Richard distractedly rolls a ball or marble back
and forth across the floor to his four-year-old son, at the same time
going on with his drinking and talking; or he casually beckons to
his son to come stand between his knees and, with one hand
around the child's waist, the other around a can of beer, he goes
on talking.

The easy manner with which the fathers manage these intimacies suggests that they have occurred before. But the child does
not manage them casually. He is excited by these intimacies, and
the clear delight he takes from them suggests that he assigns to
them a special quality and that they are by no means routine. Indeed, physical contact between father and son seems generally to
be infrequent. When it does take place, it is just as likely to be a
slap as a caress.

Compared with fathers who live with their children, separated
fathers who remain in touch with their children speak about them
more often and show them more warmth when father and child
are together. For separated fathers, the short, intermittent contacts
with their children are occasions for public display of parental tenderness and affection. When Bess brought the baby along on her
money-collecting visits to the Carry-out, she and Tally would

sometimes remain on the corner with Tally holding the baby in his arms, cooing at or nuzzling the baby as he and Bess talked. On a Saturday morning, after a visit from his wife, Stoopy stands on the corner with three other men, watching his wife disappear down the street with their two school-age children on either side of her. "There goes my heart," says Stoopy "those two kids, they're my heart." The other men nod understandingly. They would have felt and said the same thing had they been in his place.

These are fathers whose children are raised by the mothers. Even closer to his child is the father whose child is raised by the father's mother or members of his family. For him, too, the child is "my heart," "my life," or "the apple of my eye." Parental pride and affection are even more in public evidence when father and child are together. When Tonk's daughter arrives for her summer stay, Tonk walks around holding her hand, almost parading, stopping here and there to let bystanders testify that they didn't know Tonk had such a pretty girl, such a smart girl, or a girl who has grown so much so quickly. No, Sweets won't be at the Carry-out tomorrow afternoon, he has to take his daughter shopping for some clothes. He swears he didn't recognize her when his mother first walked up with her. It hadn't even been a year and he almost didn't know his own kid. If she hadn't called him "Daddy" he would still not have known, that's how big she got. And (with pride), she wants to be with him all the time she's here, go everywhere he goes.

But after the brief visit is over, each goes back to his own life, his own world, in which the other plays so small a part that he may be forgotten for long stretches of time. "Out of sight, out of mind" is not far off the mark—at least for the fathers—in these separated father-child relationships.

There are many ways to explain this paradox in which fathers who live with their children appear to be less warm, tender and affectionate in their face-to-face relationships with their children than separated fathers.[3] The most obvious, perhaps, is that the separated father, like the proverbial doting grandfather or favorite uncle, not charged with the day-to-day responsibility for the child, with the routine rearing and disciplining and support of this child, can afford to be attentive and effusive. Since his meetings with the child are widely spaced, he comes to them fresh and rested; since the meetings are brief, he can give freely of himself, secure in the knowledge he will soon go back to his own childfree routine.

No doubt, factors such as these are at work here and do account, in part, for the differences between fathers living with and those not living with their children. But one of the most striking things about the relationship between the streetcorner men and children is that the closest of all relationships are those where the men do live with the children, where they have accepted day-to-day responsibility for the children, but where they have done so on a voluntary basis, that is, where the children are not their own.

Not all streetcorner men who took on the role of stepfather or adoptive father were able or even attempted to establish a warm personal relationship with the children they were living with, but some of them were better able to achieve and sustain such relationships than any of the biological fathers. Thus, Robert, who had been living with Siserene and her four children for a year and a half, had become, in that time, a primary source of aid and comfort to the children. When they fell or were hit or had an object of value taken from them, they ran to Robert if he was there. He comforted them, laughed with them, and arbitrated their disputes. He painted pictures for them, made plywood cutouts of the Seven Dwarfs for them, and brought home storybooks.

Before and after Leroy and Charlene had their own child,

---

3. Since the attempt here is to sort out the different streetcorner father-child relationships rather than to judge them, it is not relevant that the father's willingness to remain with his children and support them, day in, day out, may be a better measure of the man as father than his expressive behavior in his face-to-face contacts with his children.

Leroy looked after Charlene's little sisters and brother to such an extent that both their mother and the children themselves came to rely on him. Together with Calvin, a frail and ailing forty-year-old alcoholic and homosexual who looked after the children in exchange for a place to live, Leroy bathed the children, braided the girls' hair, washed their clothes at "the Bendix" (laundromat), played with them, and on their birthdays went shoplifting to get them gifts. Even more than to Leroy, the children were attached to Calvin. When he could summon the courage, Calvin often interceded on their behalf when their mother was dealing out punishment. There was little that Calvin did not do for the children. He played with them during the day when they were well and stayed up with them at night when they were sick. During one period, when he had resolved to stop his homosexual practices (he had been married and a father), he resumed them only on those occasions when there was no food or money in the house and only long enough to "turn a trick" and get food for the children. When this did not work he raided the Safeway, despite his terror of still another jail sentence. He was proud of the part he played in their lives and he played it so well that the children took his love and support for granted.

It would seem, then, that differences in father-child relationships do not depend so much on whether the man is in continuous as against intermittent or occasional contact with the child but on whether the man voluntarily assumes the role of father or has it thrust upon him.

The man who lives with his wife and children is under legal and social constraints to provide for them, to be a husband to his wife and a father to his children. The chances are, however, that he is failing to provide for them, and failure in this primary function contaminates his performance as father in other respects as well. The more demonstrative and accepting he is of his children, the greater is his public and private commitment to the duties and responsibilities of fatherhood; and the greater his commitment, the greater and sharper his failure as the provider and head of the family. To soften this failure, and to lessen the damage to his public and self-esteem, he pushes the children away from him, saying, in effect, "I'm not even trying to be your father so now I can't be blamed for failing to accomplish what I'm not trying to do."

For the father separated from his children, there is no longer the social obligation to be their chief support. His performance as father is no longer an issue. His failure is an accomplished fact. But now that he is relatively free of the obligations of fatherhood, he can, in his intermittent contacts with his children, by giving money for their support and by being solicitous and affectionate with them, enjoy a modest success as father in precisely those same areas in which he is an established failure.

This is even more clearly seen in the man who lives with a woman who has had children by another man. For these men, obligations to the children are minor in comparison with those of fathers living with their children. Where the father lives with his own children, his occasional touch or other tender gesture is dwarfed by his unmet obligations. No matter how much he does, it is not enough. But where the man lives with children not his own, every gentleness and show of concern and affection redounds to his public and private credit; everything is profit. For him, living with children is not, as it is for the father, charged with failure and guilt. Since his own and others' expectations of him as father are minimal, he is free to enter into a close relationship with the children without fear of failure and uninhibited by guilt. It is as if living with your own children is to live with your failure, but to live with another man's children is, so far as children are concerned, to be in a fail-proof situation: you can win a little or a lot but, however small your effort or weak your performance, you can almost never lose.[4]

---

4. Unless, of course, the man violates the ordinary decencies of everyday life and goes out of his way to abuse the child.

In addition to the very gross factors so far considered in father-child relationships, any one of a number of other factors may pull father and child closer together or push them further apart.[5] Looking only at separated fathers, for example, who are in the majority on the streetcorner, it seems as if their relationships with their children depend to a striking degree on the father's relationships with the adult who is taking care of the child. Thus, as has been suggested earlier, fathers (e.g., Tonk and Sweets) whose children are living with the father's mother or other members of his family seem to be closer to their children than those (e.g., Sea Cat, Stoopy) whose children are living with the mother or members of her family. And when the child is with its mother, as in the great majority of cases, the frequency of contact between father and child clearly depends more on the father's relationship with the mother than on his relationship with the child himself. It is almost as if the men have no direct relationship with their children independent of their relationship with the mother. Whether in different states or in different sections of the same city, these children are never sent to spend a weekend, a Sunday, or even a few hours

---

5. For example, the child's sex, age or skin color; whether or not he is legitimate; number, sex and relative age and skin color of siblings; age and marital status of the father; literacy of father, child or other concerned adults (for written communications); accessibility or physical distance of separation, personality variables and so forth. The data generally are too thin to permit an assignment of relative weight to these but the evidence does suggest that no one of them is an overriding or controlling factor in the relationship. Among these factors, however, skin color appears to be one of the most important, the light-skinned child being preferred to the child with dark skin. There is also a clear preference for the legitimate child but, by itself, illegitimacy is no bar to a close father–child relationship. Sex of the child is important to some men but some seem to prefer boys, others girls. Most of the closest father–child relationships I have observed were with daughters but the total numbers are too few and the number of other variables too many to warrant even a tentative generalization. For a discussion of skin color in parent-child relationships, see St. Clair Drake and Horace Cayton, *Black Metropolis*, pp. 498ff, esp. p. 503. Morris Rosenberg's study of New York State school children offers strong evidence that lower-class fathers tend to be closer to their daughters than to their sons (*Society and the Adolescent Self-Image*, p. 42ff).

alone with their fathers. If, like Earl, the father does visit the child's household, it is primarily to see the mother rather than the child. As a rule, children born of short-term unions see their fathers only if and when the father and mother maintain or reestablish a personal relationship.

The dependence of the father-child on the father-mother relationship is clearly evident in the follow-up of Tally's relationship with Bess and their son. We have here, too, a picture of the way in which the father-child relationship can change over time.

After the birth of their baby, and after she and Tally had stopped going out together, Bess came to the corner only on Tally's pay day (Wednesdays), sometimes bringing the child along, sometimes not. But as Bess and Tally rediscovered their attraction for each other, she began to bring the baby regularly, coming now on Friday or Saturday evenings and sleeping over with the baby in Tally's room until Sunday night or Monday morning. On these weekends, Tally sometimes took the boy into the Carry-out shop for a soda or, on one occasion, marched up the street with the child on his shoulder, proudly announcing that Bess had "sent the men to get a loaf of bread." But after a few weeks, Tally and Bess had a fight. Bess stayed away from the neighborhood, and Tally's contacts with his son—dependent as they were on his relationship with Bess—ended abruptly.

The incidental, derivative character of the father-child relationship is not something which arises only after the birth of the child and the separation of the parents. It is rooted in values which, even before conception, boldly and explicitly assert the primacy of the man-woman relationship over a possible father-child relationship, and this primacy continues in effect over the actual father-child relationship when a child is born.

Although the relationship with children is secondary to the man-woman relationship, streetcorner men do want children quite apart from the generalized desire to have a family and be the head of it. A man who has no children may want a child to confirm his masculinity; another may want his girl or wife to conceive in order to reduce the chances of her "cheating" or "cutting out"; and still another man may want a particular woman to have his baby because this may guarantee a continuing relationship with this woman.

Fathers and nonfathers alike also see children as liabilities. The principal liability is the financial one. On the one hand, everyone agrees that a man ought to support his children; on the other hand, money is chronically in short supply. To the men, including those who do not, in fact, contribute to their children's support, children are real, imagined, or pretended economic liabilities. Having to buy food, shoes, clothes or medicine for a child, or having to make a support payment, serve equally well as reason or excuse for asking to borrow money or refusing to lend any. Everywhere one turns, the consensus is that "Children, they'll snatch a lot of biscuits off the table [children are expensive]." So and so had a baby? "Children, they'll snatch a lot of biscuits off the table." So and so is shacking up with a woman with three kids? "Children, they'll snatch a lot of biscuits off the table."

The more the children, of course, the greater the liability. Sweets says he met a girl he likes so much that he is thinking of moving in with her "even though she's got two kids." Bernard doesn't want his girl to have any more children because "I got more than I can stand [economically] right now."

Children—one's own as well as someone else's—are also seen as liabilities in the all-important world of man–woman relationships. Where eating, sleeping, child rearing and lovemaking are frequently confined to a single room, children render privacy a scarce commodity. Not only do they constitute a standing deterrent to secrecy (so essential to the maintenance of clandestine relationships) but they may severely limit the man's freedom of action in other ways as well.

Tonk, for example, made no secret of the fact that having his seven-year-old daughter with him for the summer was not an unmixed blessing. Tonk and his wife Pearl had no children. Pearl wanted the child to remain with them permanently but Tonk insisted on her returning to his mother in the fall, complaining that he has to take care of his daughter when Pearl is not home (she worked nights), and that to do this on a year-round basis would seriously compromise his freedom.

Tonk knew whereof he spoke. A few days later, on a Saturday night while Pearl was at work, Tonk went for a ride with William and two women, taking his daughter with him. The next day, serious trouble arose when the little girl pointed to one of the women and told Pearl, "She's the one who was in my daddy's arms."

Children threaten not only exposure of illicit relationships but also active interference. Indeed, when Tonk and Earlene were kissing in the car, his daughter kept trying to pull them apart, screaming at Earlene "You're not my mother! You're not my mother!"[6]

Older children, in this respect, are bigger nuisances. Clarence lived with his wife and children but saw a great deal of Nancy. Their relationship was a stormy one. Once, when Nancy and Clarence were fighting, Nancy's twelve-year-old son hit Clarence with a baseball bat. This occasioned no surprise to the men on the street and little sympathy for Clarence. The slapstick aspects of it aside, most of the men merely shrugged their shoulders. After all, it was common knowledge that a liaison with a woman who has a half-grown son is a dangerous one. Clarence had gone into it with his eyes open.

Women are painfully aware that men see children as liabilities and that a woman who has children may find it difficult to establish a satisfactory relationship with a man. Richard and Shirley are

---

6. Of course, Pearl was not her mother either. I assume that the child was using "mother" here to mean father's wife or stepmother. My notes do not say whether the child called Pearl "Mama." I would guess not since they were together only during the summer.

having a fight and Richard has told Shirley she is free to take the children and leave. Shirley is crying hard:

> Where can I go? To my mother's grave? To the D.C. morgue where they burned [cremated] my sister last month? You know I'm all alone, so where can I go? Nobody wants a woman with three babies.[7]

Lorena voices a sentiment widespread among women in her contemptuous assessment of men as fathers. In a kitchen discussion with Shirley and Charlene, she dismisses men's protests of love and concern for their children by citing their failure to follow through in action and concludes that, in fact, men regard children as liabilities.

> They [men] say they love them. Shit. If they love them, would they let them go hungry? In raggedy-ass clothes? They don't love them. Children are just a tie to a man.

Women are especially resentful of men's instrumental use of children, their use of children as tools for punishment or control in the man-woman relationship.[8] The mother-child relationship, generally conceded to be far closer than the bond between father and children, renders the mother especially vulnerable to such tactics. One woman dreads a fight with her husband because the children will suffer for it. She knows and he knows that he can "get" her by slapping the children around. Another woman, separated from her husband, gets only occasional financial support from him but she is afraid to take him to court for fear that, in order to get back at her, he would go to jail rather than send her money for the

---

7. Other things being equal, children also compromise the market value of the working- or middle-class widow or divorcee.

8. A practice which tends to support the argument of the primacy of the man-woman over the father-child relationship.

children. Leroy regularly uses his small son Donald as a sword of Damocles to control Charlene. Sometimes, during the course of a fight, he denies that Donald is his son and, secure in the knowledge that she has no place to go, he throws Charlene and the child, together with their belongings, out of the apartment (room). When the initiative lies with Charlene and she, in turn, threatens to leave him, Leroy forces her to remain by refusing to let her take the child. At other times he simply threatens to take Donald "back home" and give him to his grandmother to raise.

The widespread acknowledgment that the mother's attachment for the child is greater than the father's also provides the logical justification for assigning to the father (in theory) the role of principal disciplinarian. Responsibility for meting out physical punishment theoretically falls to the man because mothers are inhibited from punishing their children by virtue of being mothers.

"The man is way more important in bringing up a child," one man said, explaining that the father can discourage wrongdoing with a slap or a beating. Not so the woman. "The woman—well, she birthed him and she can't bring herself to hurt her baby, no matter what he does."

Men's assertions that their wives are "too easy" on the children are commonplace. "She's too easy, always kissing him and picking him up. She doesn't care if he keeps shittin' and pissin' on the floor." Tally, separated from his wife and children, continues to complain that his wife never whips them. "She's always hugging them and talking to them but sometimes they ain't going to learn [unless they are given a whipping]."

Women sometimes contend that a mother alone can raise children properly but they concede that, other things being equal, the children are better off when there's a man around to provide or threaten punishment. "I raised my three that way [alone], but it's better if there's a man. Children fear a man but they don't fear their mother. My son don't fear me at all."

Men see physical punishment as a necessary and proper part of child rearing. "A child, he needs it hard else he ain't going to learn" or "It's important [to hit children] to help them know right from wrong" are sentiments that all men subscribe to. But everyone agrees, too, that punishment ought to be meted out at the appropriate time. "You can't let them keep on doing bad things and then whip them for things they did a long time ago. You got to whip them when they done it, so they'll know what it's for." Society is seen as positively sanctioning physical punishment by specifying the way in which it is to be meted out. "You can hurt a child hitting him with a stick or in the eyes or his head. That's why it's against the law to do it like that. You're supposed to hit him on his thighs or something like that."

When one looks at the same men as sons rather than as fathers, the father–child relationship appears to be a far more distant one. In part, this may be due to the deterioration of the father–child relationship over time and to the different assessments that father and son make of their relationship, each from his own perspective. When the child is very young, the father may still be living with the family or, in any event, making an attempt to help out in some way. But after the father has left, as he usually does, the growing distance in time and space between father and family makes it increasingly difficult to sustain even a semblance of family ties between the man, on one hand, and his wife and children on the other. Just as Tally, or Stoopy, or any of the others do now, their own fathers probably spoke warmly of their children to their friends, admitted that they should be doing more for their children, and considered that, under the circumstances, they were "doing what I can." But from the child's point of view—and he sees even more from the vantage point of adulthood—the father is the man who ran out on his mother, his brothers and sisters and himself; who had, perhaps, to be taken to court to force him to pay a few dollars toward the support of his wife and children; and who, even when he was home, is perhaps best remembered with a switch or belt in his hand.

The men seldom refer to their fathers spontaneously. A group of men can reminisce for hours without the word being mentioned. Many men seem never to have known their fathers: "I don't remember him"; "He left [or died] before I was born," or simply, "Shit."

Sea Cat, who was born and raised in the neighborhood, and whose mother continued to live there, never mentioned his father at all. Leroy was raised by his grandparents. His mother and father lived in the same city, but Leroy, who remained close to his mother, mentions his father only to fix relationships or to set a scene.

Richard's father left the family while Richard was still a small child. His father operates a beer joint in Carolina and Richard has seen him on occasion, while passing through the town. His father has never seen Richard's wife or children. Richard and his father never did get along. "We just don't see eye to eye."

Tally's father also left his wife and children when Tally was a small child. "He was a racketeer, a gambler. He never worked a day in his life." When Tally was about nine or ten he was sent to stay with his father and stepmother in Birmingham. He doesn't remember why he was sent there or how long he remained. All he remembers is that his father once gave him a terrible beating.

Sometimes a brief encounter may throw light on both sides of the father-child relationship. In the episode reported below, we catch a glimpse of the man as son, husband and father. The contrast between the mother-son and father-son relationship is almost too sharp and clear, each terrifying in its own way.[9] Preston is in his middle thirties. Dressed in old army khakis, with his hands thrust in his pockets as he leans against a lamppost or the storefront, he is a regular fixture at the Downtown Cafe. Sometimes when the cafe

---

9. "Even among some of the poorest families, the mother's affectional life may be centered upon a son or daughter. . . . Her attitude often presents *a striking contrast to that of the father.*" (Emphasis added.) E. Franklin Frazier, *The Negro Family in the United States*, p. 468.

is short of help, Preston is called to fill in. Such was the case this day when I took a seat at the bar. Preston brought me a beer and started the conversation.

> "You know, I had a lot of trouble since I seen you last."
> "What kind of trouble?"
> "My mother died."
> "I'm sorry to hear that."
> "Yes, she died three weeks ago. I've been drinking myself to death ever since. Last week I drank up every cent I made before I got it. I don't know what to do. I've been thinking of killing myself."
> "You just need a little more time. Three weeks isn't very long for something like this. You'll straighten out."
> "Maybe I will, maybe I won't. My mother was all I had. I been thinking I'll go to the pet shop and get a cat."
> "How about your father?"
> "Fuck that mother. I don't even want to think about him."
> "Do you have any kids?"
> "What good are they? They're in Germany and Japan. I've been thinking I'll get married. But that's no good unless you get a girl who understands you."

He took a box from beneath the counter and asked me to open it. Inside was a flimsy nightgown decorated with bright-colored flowers. With tears in his eyes, he explained that he had bought this for his mother for her stay in the hospital but never got to give it to her. On the night of the day he bought it, he got a call from the Washington Hospital Center to come immediately. He ran all the way but his mother was already dead. Preston did not remember the subsequent events very clearly. He said he began drinking very heavily that night and either that same night or the next morning he had to go to the D.C. morgue to identify his mother's body. When the morgue attendant pulled the sheet back from his mother's face, Preston smashed the attendant in the mouth. He held up the scabby knuckles of his right fist as evidence.

"Why'd you hit him?"
"Because he showed me my dead mother."

4

HUSBANDS AND WIVES

A few of the streetcorner men expect to get married sooner or later. A few are married. Most of the men have tried marriage and found it wanting.

To be married is to be formally, legally married, to have a marriage certificate, to "have papers." The rights and duties conferred by marriage are clear-cut, unambiguous; they are those rights and duties set forth in the marriage vows and by the courts. Individuals may fail to exercise their rights or neglect their duties but they do not deny them.

Men and women are careful to distinguish between marriage on the one hand and "common law," "shacking up," "living with" and other consensual unions on the other. There is, of course, a large overlap. The rights and duties which attach to consensual unions are patterned after those which attach to marriage and, in practice, some consensual unions are publicly indistinguishable from marriage. There are two principal differences. First, the rights and duties of consensual unions generally have less public force behind them. The result is that an act which violates both the marital and consensual union invokes a stronger sanction in the case of marriage. A second difference is that, in consensual unions, rights and duties are less clearly defined, especially at the edges. The result is that while everyone would agree that a given act stands in violation of the marital relationship, there could be—and frequently is—widespread disagreement as to whether the same act stands in violation of a consensual union.

The right to exclusive sexual access to one's spouse, for example, is freely acknowledged to be a right which attaches to marriage. But there is no consensus on sex rights in consensual unions. Some streetcorner men feel that a partner in a consensual union has a right to demand exclusive sexual access; others deny this. Perhaps the majority feel that one has a right to expect sexual exclusiveness but not to demand it. Indeed, this may be the chief distinction between rights in marriage and rights in consensual union. In marriage, one partner has a legal right to demand some kinds of behavior and the other has a legal duty to perform them. In consensual union, this relationship is watered down; one partner may come to expect some kinds of behavior but the other does not have a legal duty to perform them.[1]

The distinction between the demand rights of marriage and the privilege rights of the consensual union, as well as the absence of clearly defined rights in the consensual union, can be seen in the conflict between Stanton and Bernice. Shortly after they began living together, Stanton was arrested and jailed for thirty days. Upon his release, he went to their apartment where he discovered Bernice with another man. Over the next several weeks, Stanton refused to look for work. It was understood that he was "making Bernice pay" for what she had done by forcing her to "pay the rent and buy the groceries." Had Stanton and Bernice been married, some might have questioned the wisdom or efficacy or even fairness of Stanton's action but no one would have questioned his right to do this. But Stanton and Bernice were not married and

---

1. In the language of Wesley Newcombe Hohfeld, the difference is between demand right—duty in one relationship, and privilege right—no demand right in the other. See E. Adamson Hoebel, *The Law of Primitive Man: A Study in Comparative Legal Dynamics*, pp. 48ff.

there were both men and women who said that this was a "terrible" thing for Stanton to do, that maybe Bernice hadn't done the "right" thing but she had a right to do what she did because they weren't married and, because they weren't married, what she had done had not "hurt" Stanton, and even if it had, he had no right to make her "pay" for it.

A partner to a consensual union may explicitly point out the distinction between their own relationship and marriage in order to challenge the other's right or as justification for his own behavior. Thus, one woman walked away in a huff from a man who was trying to get her to accompany him with the reminder that "I'm your girl friend, not your wife." And Leroy, at a time when he had been living with Charlene for several months, conceded that his rights were compromised by the fact that they were not formally, legally married. They had had an argument which brought their relationship almost to the breaking point. Later the same day Leroy left a note for Charlene which concluded: "I have decided to let you think it over until 6 P.M. Sunday. Until then, you can go where you want to, do what you want to, because like you said, I don't have any papers on you yet."[2]

The distinction between marriage and consensual union is also carefully drawn in the labels one applies to the incumbents in the two relationships. The terms husband and wife, for example, are almost always reserved for formally married persons. Thus, Sea Cat explains that "Priscilla is my old lady. My wife lives over in Northeast." Tally explains to William that "Sara is Budder's old lady, they ain't married." When not used for contrastive purposes, however, "old man" and "old lady" and "man" and "woman" may also be used to label husband and wife. "My old man (lady)," then, may mean either "the man (woman) I am formally, legally married to," or "the man (woman) I am living with but whom I

---

2. The time of this episode (October 1962) is especially significant. Charlene was then in her ninth month with Leroy's child but even the imminence of parenthood could not elevate their respective rights and duties to those of husband and wife.

am not formally, legally married to." But "my husband (wife)" almost always means "the man (woman) I am formally, legally married to."

These labels and their usages reflect the overlapping relationship of marriage and the consensual union. The fact that "old man" and "old lady" are equally applicable in either relationship testifies to an equivalence between marriage and consensual unions; the fact that "husband" and "wife" are reserved for marriage and denied to persons in consensual union demonstrates the distinctiveness of the marriage relationship.

Thus marriage, as compared with consensual union, is clearly the superior relationship. Marriage has higher status than consensual union and greater respectability. Not only are its rights and duties better defined and supported with greater public force but only through marriage can a man and woman lay legitimate claim to being husband and wife.

But as the man on the streetcorner looks at the reality of marriage as it is experienced day in and day out by husbands and wives, his universe tells him that marriage does not work. He knows that it did not for his own mother and father and for the parents of most of his contemporaries. He knows that Lonny strangled his wife and almost paid with his own life as well. He sees Clarence trying to keep his wife from getting at the woman she has found him with while two of their four children look on in frightened silence. He knows that Tom Tom, whose busboy job did not pay enough to support his wife and children, moved away from his family so they would become eligible for ADC. He sees Leroy and Charlene circling slowly on the sidewalk, with Charlene holding a broken Coke bottle thrust in front of her and Leroy pawing at her with his right arm wrapped in his jacket. He sees Tonk standing on the corner where his wife works as a waitress, afraid himself to take a job because the word is going around that she is "cutting out" on him. He sees Shirley bury her face in her hands and shudder, partly perhaps because the Christmas wind has again ripped away the blanket nailed across the window but mainly because she and Richard are trying to decide whether to send the children to Junior Village[3] or take them to the waiting room at Union Station for the night. And at two in the morning, he sees Leroy and Charlene, with Leroy holding their year-old son in his arms, anxiously looking for someone, anyone, to take them to Children's Hospital because their sleeping baby had just been bitten on the cheek by a rat.

These are the things he sees and hears and knows of street-corner marriage: the disenchantment, sometimes bitter, of those who were or still are married; the public and private fights between husband and wife and the sexual jealousy that rages around them; husbands who cannot feed, clothe and house their wives and children and husbands who have lost their will to do so; the terror of husband and wife who suddenly find themselves unable to ward off attacks on the health and safety of their children. Nor is there—to redeem all this even in part—a single marriage among the streetcorner men and their women which they themselves recognize as a "good" marriage.

The talk that the streetcorner man is exposed to is uniformly antimarriage. On the corner, he hears Sea Cat proclaim that "I was married once and once was enough," and he hears a chorus of assent from the others: "I'll go along with that," they say. In the privacy of Richard's room, Richard, speaking quietly and with feeling, tells him that if his marriage to Shirley breaks up, "later for a marriage,[4] man, I don't want to get married again."

He hears others question whether Sea Cat or Richard or any other man really wanted to get married in the first place. They ascribe marriage to a variety of precipitating incidents and circumstances which are seen as pushing the man into marriage against his will. This presumption of coercion may apply to one's own

---

3. Washington, D.C.'s home for neglected and dependent children.
4. "Later for [something]" means roughly, I do not want anything to do with or I am not concerned with that something, at least for the present.

marriage as well as to others. Richard usually claimed that he married Shirley only because his grandmother promised him fifty dollars if he would do so. The men generally agreed that if Leroy ever married Charlene (which he finally did), it would only be because Charlene had his baby and because Charlene's mother, Malvina, and her social worker were "getting behind him" (i.e., putting pressure on him). The men said that Robert married Siserene only to meet the competition from Lonny who had himself offered to marry her to get her away from Robert.

Where coercion cannot be presumed, the men claim not to understand the motive for marriage at all. When word reached the corner that Boley was to be married that weekend, Tonk shook his head and said he didn't understand why Boley was getting married since he was already shacking up with the girl anyway. No one else admitted to understanding it, either. Along with the others, Richard believed coercion to be an especially important element in early marriages.

> The average person you see at eighteen, he don't have nothing of his own and he gets out there [into the world]. And the average person you see now that gets married at eighteen, he gets married because they're gonna have a kid or something.

But the closer one looks at the individual cases, the more difficult it is to detect coercion. Robert was admittedly under no pressure at all. Siserene had, in fact, already decided against marrying Lonny and had gone back to living with Robert when Robert asked her to marry him. As for Leroy, it is true that he was under pressure from Malvina, her social worker, and the people at the clinic where Charlene went for prenatal care, but Charlene gave Leroy many opportunities to get out from under—had he chosen to do so—by saying she preferred to postpone the marriage until after the baby was born so that Leroy could make his decision free of external pressures.[5]

Thus, the contention that many men are, like Leroy, forced into marriage by premarital births or pregnancies is at best a half-truth for the men on the streetcorner, most of whom fathered one or more children before marriage by women other than those they subsequently married. It is true that the man usually feels a strong obligation to both the woman and the children she bears him and, on occasion, even an obligation to marry the woman if she's amenable to marriage. But if for any reason he is simply not ready to marry this woman, he does not. Like Tonk, he may take the child, give it to his mother, and contribute to its support; like Tommy, he may remain friends with the woman and help her financially whenever he can; like William, he may simply take off for parts unknown. If, like Wesley, he feels guilty about not marrying her, it is a guilt he can live with.

> The girl [mother of Wesley's child] . . . she's ready to get married any time I say so. . . . Right now, this girl—as long as this girl's single, I'm not going to get married. I don't want to marry her and I don't want to marry nobody else until she gets married. You see, when she gets married, I figure I'm free. You see, if I get married, I'd be inclined to think me awhile. I think about it now. I say, "I should go and marry this girl." But I don't want to.

Thus, the presumption of coercion in marriage is, in part at least, a public fiction. Beneath the pose of the put-upon male, and obscured by it, is a generalized readiness to get married, a readiness based principally on the recognition of marriage as a rite through which one passes into man's estate. For the young, never-married male, to get married is to become a man.

---

5. In fact, they did not get married until July 1964 when their son was a year and a half old and Charlene was several months pregnant with their second child.

> It was a big deal when I got married. I didn't have to get married. We didn't have no children or nothing. But you know, I gonna be—try to prove I'm a man or something, and I jump up and get married. . . .

Richard said this softly, in a matter-of-fact tone, as he spoke to Wesley and me of his marriage.[6] Wesley nodded. He knew what Richard meant. He said he wanted to marry and settle down, too. He had the girl all picked out and was just waiting for the other girl by whom he had had a child to marry. Earl and Boley and the other young never-married men had not fixed on a girl or a time but privately they assumed they would be getting married soon, too.

The discrepancy between the private readiness to marry and the public presumption of coercion points up the discrepancy between what marriage is supposed to be and what it is, in fact. In theory, marriage is "a big thing"; it is the way to manhood with all its attendant responsibilities, duties, and obligations which, when discharged, bring one status and respectability. In fact, marriage is an occasion of failure in the critical area of manhood, and therefore leads to a diminished status and loss of respectability. The difference between what marriage offers in theory and what it delivers in fact can be as dust in one's mouth. It was in Richard's.

> A man [ready to get married], he's got big ideas. He thinks marriage is a big thing, you know. But you know, it's no big thing.

Men may want "to jump up and get married," "to be a man or something," but knowing, or strongly suspecting, that marriage is a poor risk, they hedge against probable failure by camouflaging their private readiness to marry with the public fiction of coercion.

---

6. This time, there was no boastful reference to his grandmother and the fifty dollar bribe—an omission which suggests that the bribe served mainly as an enabling mechanism for his own readiness to marry.

Hedging takes the edge off failure. The hedge asserts that the man does not enter fully and freely into the marriage contract; that he was forced into it, went into it reluctantly, or was merely "going along with the program." Thus, marriage becomes, in part, a hold that is not a hold. The hedge permits a more passive participation than the obligation that total public commitment carries with it. It gives the man a partial defense against those who would hold him strictly to the terms of the contract; and it somewhat lightens the onus attached to breaking up the marriage by permitting him to say, in effect, "I didn't really want to get married in the first place."

WHY MARRIAGE DOES NOT WORK

The Theory of Manly Flaws—As the men look back on their broken marriages, they tend to explain the failure in terms of their personal inability or unwillingness to adjust to the built-in demands of the marriage relationship. Sea Cat, for example, admits to a group of men on the corner that his marriage broke up because he simply could not bring himself to subordinate his independence to the demands of a joint undertaking.

> I was married once and once was enough. I can't live that way, having someone tell me when to get up, when to eat, "go here," "go there." Man, I've got to be master. I've got to be kingpin.[7]

Stoopy blamed the failure of his marriage on his weakness for whiskey and would tell how angry his wife used to become when he got drunk and spent or gambled away the rent money. She put up with him longer than he had a right to expect her to, he said. Even now, when she comes on Saturday mornings to pick up money for the children, she says she is willing to try again if he

---

7. Women, too, want the man to be "master," but the word means one thing to husbands, another to wives. See p. 85.

will promise never to get drunk but he knows he could not stick to such a promise, even though he loves her and the children and would like them to get back together.

Stoopy, like Sea Cat, showed no rancor when his wife took him to court for nonsupport. Stoopy and Sea Cat had let their wives down; they were the ones who had violated the marital agreement and their wives were doing what they had a perfect right to do.

Tally felt much the same way. When he was living with his wife, his drinking and "bad language" rightly disturbed her. Also, he couldn't stay away from other women. But he still loved her and if she would give him another chance, he would "put down" all those things which come so easily to a man but which a wife is justified in refusing to accept in a husband.

> . . . I love my wife. When I go to bed at night [it's as if] she's with me, and my kids are, too. Deep down in my heart, I believe she's coming back to me. I really believe it. And if she do, I'm going to throw out all these other women. I'm going to change my whole life.

On close inspection, it is difficult to accept these self-analyses of marital failure at full face value. Quite apart from the fact that it seems to be the men who leave their wives, rather than the other way around, these public assumptions of blame express a modesty that is too self-serving to be above suspicion. In each instance, the man is always careful to attribute his inadequacies as a husband to his inability to slough off one or another attribute of manliness, such as independence of spirit, a liking for whiskey, or an appetite for a variety of women. They trace their failures as husbands directly to their weaknesses as men, to their manly flaws.[8]

Simple and self-serving, this theory of manly flaws to account

---

8. ". . . people do not simply want to excel; they want to excel as a man or as a woman, that is to say, in those respects which, in their culture, are symbolic of their respective sex roles. . . . Even when they adopt behavior which is considered disrepu-

for the failure of marriage has a strong appeal for the men on the streetcorner.[9] But the theory is too pat, too simple; one senses that it violates the principle of sufficient cause. The relational complexities of marriage and its breakdown want answers which touch on these complexities. A more detailed examination of sexual infidelity—the largest and most common manly flaw—suggests that these flaws are not too damaging in themselves but that each is rooted in a host of antecedents and consequences which reach into the very stuff of marriage.

Sexual Infidelity as a Manly Flaw—Tally's contention that he would "throw out all those women" if his wife would only return to him was acceptable as a declaration of good intentions, but none of the men on the streetcorner would accept it as a description of what would happen in fact. One of the most widespread and strongly supported views the men have of themselves and others is that men are, by nature, not monogamous; that no man can be satisfied with only one woman at a time.[10] This view holds that, quite apart from his desire to exploit women, the man seeks them out because it is his nature to do so. This "nature" that shapes his sex life, however, is not human nature but rather an animality which the

---

table by conventional standards, *the tendency is to be disreputable in ways that are characteristically masculine and feminine.*" (Emphasis added.) Albert K. Cohen, *Delinquent Boys*, p. 138.

9. In an imaginative discussion of adaptations to failure in the evolution of delinquent subcultures, Cloward and Ohlin hypothesize that "collective adaptations are likely to emerge where failure is attributed to the inadequacy of existing institutional arrangements; conversely, when failure is attributed to personal deficiencies, solitary adaptations are more likely." Richard A. Cloward and Lloyd E. Ohlin, *Delinquency and Opportunity: A Theory of Delinquent Gangs*, p. 125. The "theory of manly flaws," when seen as an adaptation to failure in marriage, does not appear to fit this hypothesis, or at least suggests another possibility: a collective adaptation in which the participants agree to attribute failure to themselves as individuals.

10. "In lower social levels there is a somewhat bitter acceptance of the idea that the male is basically promiscuous and that he is going to have extramarital intercourse, whether or not his wife or society objects." Alfred C. Kinsey, Wardell B. Pomeroy, and Clyde E. Martin, "Social Level and Sexual Outlet," p. 307.

human overlay cannot quite cover. The man who has a wife or
other woman continues to seek out others because he has too
much "dog" in him.

> Men are just dogs! We shouldn't call ourselves human, we're
> just dogs, dogs, dogs! They call me a dog, 'cause that's what I am,
> but so is everybody else—hopping around from woman to woman,
> just like a dog.

This pronouncement from Sea Cat met with unanimous agreement from the men on the corner. Another occasion brought forth
similar unanimity. It was a Friday evening. Tally, Clarence, Preston, Wee Tom and I were sitting in a parked car and drinking.
Tally cooed at the women as they walked by.

One woman, in response to Tally's "Where you going, baby?"
approached the car and looked the five of us over carefully, each
in turn. "Walking," she said, and turned away. We watched her
saunter across the street, her hips lurching from side to side as if
they were wholly independent of the rest of her body. "That's real
nice," said Tally, "that's real nice." There was a chorus of yes
noises from the others.

I wondered aloud at the paradox of the five of us, each with a
good woman waiting for him to come home (although Tally was
living alone at the time), sitting in a car, drinking, and ready to
take on any woman who walked down the street. The answer
came quickly, unanimously: we (men) have too much dog in us.

"It don't matter how much a man loves his wife and kids,"
said Clarence, "he's gonna keep on chasing other women. . . . A
man's got too much dog in him." The others agreed with Clarence and remained in complete agreement throughout the discussion which followed.[11]

---

11. But a few minutes later, when the question arose as to whether women have
as much dog in them as men, the men were less sure of their answers and disagreed
among themselves. One said that women have as much dog in them as men but that

The dog in man which impels him to seek out an ever-expanding universe of sex is a push-pull affair. A "new" woman is, by common consent, more stimulating and satisfying sexually than one's own wife or girl friend. The man also sees himself performing better with "new meat" or "fresh meat" than with someone familiar to him sexually. Men in their late twenties or older pooh-pooh the suggestion that they are not as good sexually as they were in their late teens or early twenties, maintaining that their performance in any given sex encounter depends less on age or any other personal factor than on the woman they happen to be with. Variety is not only the spice of sex life, it is an aphrodisiac which elevates the man's sexual performance. The point is perhaps best made by a standard joke which frequently appeared when the subject of sexual competence came up. It was told more as a fact of life than as a subject of humor.

> An old man and his wife were sitting on their porch, rocking slowly and watching a rooster one hen, then another. When the rooster had repeated this performance several times, the old woman turned to her husband and said, "Why can't you be like that rooster?"
>
> "If you look close," the old man said, "you'll see that that rooster ain't knockin' off the same hen each time. If he had to stick with the same one, he wouldn't do no better than me."

In attempting to sustain simultaneous relationships with one's wife and one or more other women, it frequently happens that one such relationship compromises the other. The marriage rela-

---

a good woman also has a lot of pride and that's what keeps her from acting the same way men do. Another said that women have less dog in them, hence their more conservative sexual behavior. A third opinion held that women had more dog than men but that this was obscured by the double standard which inhibited women's freedom of action. And still another held that some women have less dog than men, some more, and that this accounted for the division of women into "good" and "bad."

tionship, in particular, may suffer sexual damage. The man who admits this is not thereby diminished. He does not have to—nor does he—boast of the frequency with which he can engage in sex nor of the number of times he can achieve an orgasm in any given encounter. In special circumstances, he can even admit to not being able to engage in sex and, in doing so, enhance his image as a man who is successful with women. This is the case, for example, when the men talk about coming home from an engagement with another woman and being unable or unwilling to meet the sexual demands of their wives or women they are living with.

This predicament is freely admitted to in an almost boastful manner. On the streetcorner, it is a source of great merriment, with each man claiming to have a characteristic way of dealing with it. Sea Cat claims that he usually feigns sleep or illness; Clarence insists on staying up to watch the late show on TV, waiting for his wife to give up and go to sleep; Richard manufactures an argument and sleeps anywhere but in bed with Shirley; others feign drunkenness, job exhaustion, or simply stay away from home until their wives are asleep or until morning when the household is up and beginning another day.

The damage inflicted on marriage by such avoidance behavior tends to be assessed one way by men, another by women. The man tends to look at the problem in simple terms: he has a flaw which leads him to run around with other women. He simply has too much dog in him. True, he has violated the marriage, but only in this one narrow area of sexual fidelity.

In fact, the damage is much wider and deeper, as suggested by the wife in one of the streetcorner marriages that was falling apart. In bitterness mixed with resignation, she told of how her husband had been running around with other women and avoiding her sexually. She could live with this, she said, but what made the situation intolerable was his determination to find fault with everything she did, such as the way she cared for the children or cleaned the room. What started out as a transparent attempt to create arguments as an excuse for avoiding sex with her had gotten out of hand.[12] The result, she said, was that all areas of their life, not only the sexual, were being poisoned.

Holding the narrow viewpoint implicit in the theory of manly flaws can lead to a false statement of the problem and to irrelevant solutions. Richard is a case in point. His marriage to Shirley was going badly. Almost nothing was right. The problem, as he saw it, was a simple one. "I'm a sport. I'll always be a sport. I was born that way. I got a lot of dog in me." Being a sport, he said, drove him to seek out other women. Being a "walking man" (because he had no car) forced him to confine his amorous adventures to within walking distance of home and this, in turn, led to repeated discovery by Shirley and to a home life characterized by chronic fights and arguments. Now if he had a car, he argued, he would have women outside the area. Shirley wouldn't know where he was—at least, she wouldn't catch him at it—and the fights and arguments would stop.[13]

Another Point of View—Not all the men hold to the theory of manly flaws in accounting for the failure of their marriage. Sometimes, even those who do may give alternate explanations. In general, those who do not blame themselves for the failure of their marriage blame their wives, rather than family, friends, marriage

---

12. One need not be a specialist in intrapsychic processes to recognize the snow-balling effect of guilt on the one hand, and self-justifying behavior to relieve the guilt, on the other. They feed on one another. One starts with "wrong" behavior, feels guilty for it, attempts to create, post facto, conditions which justify the original behavior, and feels guilty all over again, and so on and on.

13. Richard repeated this argument at different times, each time in complete seriousness. It is an appealing argument. If access to an automobile does indeed confer stability on marriage, then, other things being equal, working- and middle-class marriages have a better chance for survival than marriages among the lower, unpropertied classes. At best, however, it is a highly debatable point. When Richard did manage to acquire an automobile for a brief few weeks, the deterioration of his marriage to Shirley was dramatically accelerated.

itself, or the world at large. Even Richard, a prominent exponent of the theory of manly flaws, once shifted his ground. His marriage to Shirley had deteriorated to the point that it was barely recognizable as such. "I'm going to cut out," he said. "I can't take no more of her shit. She's getting under my skin."

One older man recalls in detail how his marriage ended.

> Me and my wife separated May 31, 1940, Friday night. I came home from work and right away she started nagging me. She said the landlord wanted his rent money and the insurance man, he was there too. I was tired of all that nagging. I said I had some money and she could pay the insurance man tomorrow when I went to work. I was real drunk and she hit me with brass knuckles. Then I got mad and cut her . . .[14]

Sweets's explanation was along the same lines.

> From now on, I'm playing the field. A man's better off in the field. I lived with her five years and every day, as soon as I walked in the house, I'd hear nothing but nagging. Mostly money. I got tired hearing all that shit.

Explanations such as these appear to stand up better than those which emphasize manly flaws. They are more solid on several counts. First, they suggest that it is the husband who does the leaving, which seems most often to be the case in fact. Second, they are not self-serving. True, they do place the blame on the wife but

---

14. Together with other references to violence between husband and wife, this quotation is, in my opinion, clear supporting evidence for the insightful observation that "rolling pins and pots are more often preludes to the disintegration of marriage than the basis on which a balance of power is worked out." Robert O. Blood and Donald M. Wolfe, *Husbands and Wives: The Dynamics of Married Living*, p. 12. Thus, the widespread violence between streetcorner husbands and their wives seems to be more a product of persons engaged in an always failing enterprise than merely the "style" or "characteristic feature" of streetcorner husband-wife relationships.

no special advantage accrues to the man thereby; neither his public nor private self is materially enhanced. And third, unlike the appeal to manly flaws, these explanations are compatible with the way in which women look at the same events. Both agree that the man quits, and quits under the pressure of the marriage relationship. To the man, the pressure is generated by his wife's expectations of him as a husband. Importantly, he avoids the "why" of her nagging behavior and complains of the "how." He does not deny the legitimacy of her expectations but objects to their insistent repetition and the unrelieved constancy of it all. "Getting under my skin" and nagging behavior give flesh-and-blood expression to his wife's unmet legitimate expectations for herself and her children. This, it seems, is what he finds so intolerable, for his wife's unmet expectations are a standing reminder of his failure as husband and father.

The foregoing quotations point clearly to the importance of money in the wife's expectations. To pay the rent, buy the groceries, and provide for the other necessary goods and services is the sine qua non of a good husband. There are, of course, several possible alternate sources of financial support—the wife herself, friends or relatives, or public or private agencies—but it remains peculiarly the (good) husband's responsibility, not anyone else's.[15]

---

15. Providing financial support is so intimately associated with the husband that, on one curious occasion, financial support was argued to be one of two paramount considerations in defining sex and kinship roles. Charlene was pregnant but she and Leroy were not yet married when Leroy got into a heated argument with Beverly, the bull-dagger (Lesbian) who was living with Charlene's mother, Malvina. They cursed one another and Leroy took out his knife. Beverly was indignant, and pointed out that Leroy should be more respectful because she, Beverly, was his stepfather-in-law! Her argument rested on the twin assertions that she was sleeping with Malvina and supporting her.

Beverly should have left well enough alone. Leroy was willing to acknowledge some merit in her argument but when Beverly claimed she was even more of a man than Leroy, this was too much. Laughing about it the next day, Leroy recalls what followed: "I said, 'If you're more of a man than I am, put your meat out and lay it on this rail.' I put mine on the rail and she said, 'I'm not that common. I don't do my lovin' that way.'"

The primacy ascribed to financial support derives from two analytically separable sources of value: the simple use value, in and of itself, of supporting and maintaining the lives of one's wife and children; and the expressive or symbolic value associated with providing this support.[16] Men and women both agree that providing financial support has a weightiness that goes beyond its simple use value. One of the men was talking to several others, derogating someone he didn't particularly care for. "But one thing you got to say," he conceded, "when he was living with her, he stone[17] took care of her and the children."

By itself, the plain fact of supporting one's wife and children defines the principal obligation of a husband. But the expressive value carried by the providing of this support elevates the husband to manliness. He who provides for his wife and children has gone a long way toward meeting his obligations to his family as he sees them. Drinking, gambling, or seeing other women may detract from but cannot, by themselves, nullify his performance. Both as husband and father, he has gone a long way toward proving himself a man.

Few married men, however, do in fact support their families over sustained periods of time. Money is chronically in short supply and chronically a source of dissension in the home. Financial support for herself and her children remains one of the principal

---

16. Studies of a variety of lower-class populations emphasize that, for the man, self-respect, status, self-esteem, etc., is intimately bound up with the ability to support one's family: "The man's role is financial and his status in the household depends rather stringently on his ability as a breadwinner: his self-respect is closely tied to his financial independence." Josephine Klein, *Samples from English Cultures*, Vol. I, p. 164; "A man who . . . is unable to carry out his breadwinning role . . . falls a great distance in the estimation of himself, his wife and children, and his fellows." J. H. Robb, *Working-Class Anti-Semite*, quoted in *Samples from English Cultures*, Vol. I, p. 164; "The Negro man . . . cannot provide the economic support that is a *principal male function* in American society. As a result, the woman becomes the head of the family, and the man a marginal appendage who deserts or is rejected by his wife . . ." Herbert J. Gans, "The Negro Family: Reflections on the Moynihan Report," p. 48.

17. An intensive, in this case meaning "really took care . . ."

unmet expectations of the wife. Moreover, although providing such support would be, so far as the husband is concerned, necessary and sufficient, the wife—who seldom gets even this much—wants more, much more.

She wants him to be a man in her terms, a husband and father according to her lights. It is not enough that he simply give money for her and the children's support, then step away until the next time he shares his pay day with them. She wants him to join them as a full-time member of the family, to participate in their affairs, to take an active interest in her and the children, in their activities, in their development as individuals. She wants his ultimate loyalty to be to her and the children, and she wants this loyalty to be public knowledge. She wants the family to present a united front to the outside world.

Most important of all, perhaps, she wants him to be *head of the family*, not only to take an interest and demonstrate concern but to take responsibility and to make decisions. She wants him to take charge, to "wear the pants," to lay down the rules of their day-to-day life and enforce them. She wants him to take over, to be someone she can lean on. Alas, she ends up standing alone or, even worse perhaps, having to hold him up as well.

Wryly, and with a bitterness born of experience, Shirley smiles to herself and says,

> I used to lean on Richard. Like when I was having the baby, I leaned on him but he wasn't there and I fell down . . . Now, I don't lean on him anymore. I pretend I lean, but I'm not leaning.

Shirley had not always surrendered with quiet resignation. Like Lorena and other women, she too had tried to cajole, tease, shame, encourage, threaten, or otherwise attempt to make her man a man. Lorena said that in the beginning of her marriage, she used to pray to God, "Make John a good husband and father." Then she realized that "that's not God's job, that's my job," and she changed her prayers accordingly: "Lord, this is Lorena Patterson. You know all about me. You know what I need."

So Lorena took on herself the job of making John a good husband and father, but it didn't work. She blames herself for the failure of her marriage but she blames John, too. John was a boy, she said, not a man. He wasn't the "master."

> I want the man to wear the pants but John made me wear the pants, too. His pants had a crease in them, mine had a ruffle, but I was wearing the pants, too.

Lorena's desperate gambits to force John to assert himself as man of the house ended disastrously, leaving her with mixed feelings of contempt, indignation, pity, and failure.

> After we got married, I used to push him to see how far I could go. Once, I told him to kiss my ass. He laid my lip open and I stayed in the room till the scar healed up. For the next two weeks, he didn't do anything, no matter what I did, so I tried again. I called him an s.o.b. His family used to say that those were fighting words to John. They said he couldn't stand to hear anyone say something about his mother. So I called him an s.o.b. You know what he did? He sat down in a chair and cried. He just sat down and cried!

The husband who sometimes responds to this testing and challenging by slapping his wife's face or putting his fist in her mouth is frequently surprised at the satisfactory results. He does not understand—or does not admit to understanding—the woman's motives and may attribute them to some vague impulse to masochism latent in women. Leroy, for example, was getting ready to take his leave from the streetcorner. He said he was going home to see what "Mouth" (Charlene) wanted. She probably wanted a whipping, he said; she seems to beg him to beat her. Afterwards, she's "tame as a baby, sweet as she can be."

Then he told of how, the day before, Charlene beat on him

with a broomstick, daring him to slap her, but he simply walked out because he knew this would hurt her more than a whipping. Doubtless, it did. For Charlene, like Lorena, wanted some tangible evidence that her husband cared about her, about them as a family, and that he was willing to fight to establish and protect his (nominal) status as head of the family. She openly envied Shirley who, when things were going tolerably well for her and Richard, took pleasure in boasting to Charlene, Lorena and other women that Richard pushed her around, insisted she stay off the street, and enforced the rule that she be up early every morning, dress the children and clean the house. For evidence of this kind of concern, Charlene would gladly pay the price of a slap in the face or a pushing around. All too often, however, Leroy declined to accept the challenge or, accepting it, was himself reduced, like John, to tears of shame, helplessness and defeat.

Richard and Shirley, whom Leroy and Charlene lived with for several months, were frequent observers—or rather overhearers—of these tearful denouements to Leroy and Charlene's domestic quarrels. Richard was contemptuous of Leroy. No one had ever seen Richard cry. Leroy must be "weak" or "lame" to let Charlene make him cry like that. As for himself, he cried, too, he admitted, but he always cried "on the inside."

Thus, marriage is an occasion of failure. To stay married is to live with your failure, to be confronted by it day in and day out. It is to live in a world whose standards of manliness are forever beyond one's reach, where one is continuously tested and challenged and continually found wanting. In self-defense, the husband retreats to the streetcorner. Here, where the measure of man is considerably smaller, and where weaknesses are somehow turned upside down and almost magically transformed into strengths, he can be, once again, a man among men.

5

LOVERS AND EXPLOITERS

M en and women talk of themselves and others as cynical, self-serving marauders, ceaselessly exploiting one another as use objects or objects of income.[1] Sometimes, such motives are ascribed only to women: "Them girls [whom the men on the corner hang out with], they want finance, not romance." But more often, the men prefer to see themselves as the exploiters, the women as the exploited, as in assessing a woman's desirability in terms of her wealth or earning power or in equating being "nice" with having a job. At a party, Tally waits for Jessie to arrive and grins with anticipation. "She's not pretty,"[2] he said, "but she's got a beautiful job."

---

1. This kind of exploitation was also found in a lower-class district of London where "there is also an important exploitative component in the 'love-relationship,' at least on the man's side. . . . The boy may be overtly exploitative, not only of the sexual intercourse which the girl permits, but also of what he can get out of her financially." Josephine Klein, *Samples from English Cultures*, Vol. I, p. 39.

2. Other things being equal, the more closely a woman approached her white counterpart, the more attractive she was considered to be, by both men and women alike. "Good hair" (hair that is long and soft) and light skin were the chief criteria. "Good hair" normally referred to head hair alone, but several of the men also expressed a preference for women with down on their cheeks or long leg hair. In one instance, one of the men explained his strong attraction to a woman by noting that

Lounging in the Carry-out shop, Leroy boasts to the men at the pinball machine about the girl he had recently met. She worked in a cafeteria near the hotel where he worked as a bellboy. When they went out, he said, they always used her money.

"She just got herself a government job," said Leroy. "She never misses a day's work. She's a real mule."

"Hell, who wants to live with a mule?" I asked.

"Man, that's the best thing to live with," said Leroy. "When you got somebody who can pull that wagon, you really got something." He turned to Lonny and asked if this wasn't so. Lonny agreed that it was.

Sweets similarly presented himself as an exploiter, boasting that

---

"she has hair all up and down her chest." But a light-skinned woman, while admittedly more attractive than her darker sister, was someone to be avoided, except perhaps as a partner for a couple of hours or one night. With the possible exception of Sea Cat, the men were uniformly afraid of women whose skin color was markedly lighter than one commonly saw on the street. The explanation given was simple and straightforward: "A light-skinned woman will turn on [against] you."

Sweets spoke with intense feeling on the subject. Talking about the woman he had just broken off with, he said that though they had lived together for a few weeks, he never really considered her his woman because she was "a light-skinned girl." He couldn't even like her because of it. One day, just as he knew she would, she turned on him and called him "bad names." (That is, "nigger," "black [something]" and other color slurs.) "I put my fist in her mouth. Now she's living with a friend of mine and he says she's okay. He doesn't know how she turned on me with all those bad names. He'll find out though. All of them, they'll all talk that shit if they get mad enough. And they all get mad enough sometime."

The others agreed with Sweets in principle, differing only in that some would admit there might be exceptions. Tally, Richard and I had just walked out of a beer joint and I said that the girl who served us was a good-looking woman. Tally said, "She's all right, but she's too light for me." I asked whether all light-skinned women turn on a man.

"Well, maybe not all of them, but eight out of ten of them will. You get in an argument with them and they start talking a lot of shit, calling you all kinds of names, and the first thing you know you re in the police station. Flora [an exceptionally dark-skinned woman], Flora's the kind of girl I like."

"Yeah," said Richard. "You get in an argument with a girl like Flora and she's got to stick to the subject." (That is, because Flora is dark-skinned, she is in no position to resort to color slurs and must restrict her argument to the matter at hand.)

he had a room in another section of town as well as the one near the Carry-out but pays no rent for either one. "Man, I don't pay rent in no places. My lady friends do that." And later, confronted by the choice of whether or not to move in with still another woman who had two children, he weighed aloud the advantages and disabilities. "She's real nice—works two jobs," he said, and he guessed that this would compensate for the disability presented by the children.

The men are eager to present themselves as exploiters to women as well as to men. The presence of a woman may encourage a man to an even more flamboyant portrayal of himself as the ruthless exploiter. The following (tape-recorded) exchange took place in Richard's apartment among Wesley, Richard and Richard's twenty-two-year-old half-sister Thelma, who was visiting from New York.

> WESLEY: From now [on], if a girl ain't got money and a car, I'm not talking to her.
>
> THELMA: But you don't find very many of those girls.
>
> WESLEY: My buddy next door, he's got one. She's got a '58 Mercury and I hear she's got a whole lot of money.
>
> THELMA: How old is she?
>
> WESLEY: I don't know how old she is but she sure parks that Mercury in front of that door.
>
> RICHARD: She could be sixty if she give me some of that money, let me drive that new car.[3]

---

3. Within very broad limits, a woman's chronological or relative age does not appear to be a crucial factor in assessing her potential as a sex partner. By and large, sex partners are roughly contemporaries of one another, but this is by no means the rule. The same man may be at once attracted to a girl in her middle teens and to a woman in her mid-forties, as evidenced, for example, by the fact that the mother of one of Tally's children was a teen-age girl and the mother of another of his children was herself a grandmother in her forties. Conversely, one may also find a man in his early twenties and a man in his forties competing for the favor of, say, a twenty- or thirty-year-old woman. Actions and attitudes varied greatly from individual to individual. Tally held that "a man usually likes a older head," (i.e., a woman older than himself)

WESLEY: [Agreeing vigorously] What'cha talking about, man!

THELMA: But won't you be embarrassed—to be seen with an older woman?

WESLEY: No. I was dumb one time. This lady, she was about forty-five. She got her own home. She got a white Cadillac, '60. She got a restaurant and she tried her best to talk to me. She told my landlady, told my landlady to get me to call and I wouldn't. But now let her come around! I'll tell the landlady, "Anytime she come around, call Wesley." I was crazy then. All that money! Ooh, I could play a long time! I could cool it. All that money and riding around in a big Cadillac. I'd ride the other women around.

THELMA: She'll have you fixed so you can't ride the other women around.

WESLEY: Uh-uh. I'm smarter than she is. She's got a daughter about nineteen. I'd have her daughter [too]. I'd be stone living!

Men not only present themselves as economic exploiters of women but expect other men to do the same. When other men's behavior does not meet these expectations, they claim not to understand the behavior.

Tally and I were in the Carry-out and I had just told Tally that Sea Cat said he was putting out the woman who had been living with him for the past seven months. Tally's initial disbelief dissolved into puzzlement.

> Sea Cat's just talking. He ain't puttin' her out. A bird in the hand is worth two million in the air . . . I can't understand Sea Cat. He's had lots of girls. He treats the goods ones real bad and he's real nice to the mean ones. The girl he's got now, she's real nice, she works every day . . .

---

and frequently bore this out in practice. Richard, on the other hand, notwithstanding his "she could be sixty" once "put down" a woman of thirty or so, forgoing the pleasures of her automobile as well, because "She's too old. I like tender meat."

On the corner, with three other men standing around, Sea Cat deplored the fact that not all men were users of women because those men—and he stopped to curse them—who spend money on women are "spoiling the women for the rest of us." Moreover, the thought that many women think nothing of going to "a club" and spending twenty dollars distressed him.

> "Hell, if I can get that twenty dollars, I can give them all the beer and liquor they can drink and ten dollars will still be in my pocket. They wouldn't know the difference."

Men saw themselves as users of women as sex objects as well as objects of income.[4] Where "pussy" is concerned, a man should "take what he can get when he can get it." Tally earnestly proclaimed that his own motto for dealing with women was "Everything New for '62." Similarly, Sea Cat was angered when a Friday night party at which he expected to meet several new women

---

4. The sexual exploitation of women does not refer to sex practices. The street-corner man's heterosexual sex practices are wholly compatible with the observation that "[lower-class] taboos are more often turned against . . . any substitution for simple and direct coitus. . . . [substitutes for intercourse are] considered a perversion. . . ." Kinsey, Pomeroy, and Martin, "Social Level and Sexual Outlet," p. 305. Anal and oral intercourse, for example, are thought of as belonging exclusively to the homosexual world. Even the labels or terms designating or describing cunnilinguism—used so commonly by servicemen and working-class males generally as contemptuous terms of address or in comradely jest—are very seldom used. That such practices stand in clear violation of the heterosexual relationship is strongly suggested by one of the few conversations that touched on the subject. Several of us were standing in a hallway drinking. Upstairs, we could hear an argument between a man and a woman, and the talk moved around to violence between man and wife. Stanton contributed a story about a woman who was continuously abused by her husband, who slept with a gun under his pillow. One night the man came home drunk and forced his wife to perform an "unnatural" act. When he fell asleep, she took a two-bladed axe from the kitchen and held it over his head, closed her eyes, and buried the axe in the middle of his forehead. Screaming, she ran from the house and told her story to the people in the town. She didn't ever come to trial, said Stanton, concluding his story. "They didn't even carry her to court." Tonk, Boley, and everyone else agreed that justice had been done.

failed to come off. The thought of his missed opportunities ran-
kled him all the next day. "I could have scored," he kept repeating, slamming his fist into his open hand with annoyance. "I know
I could have scored." As several other men on the corner looked
on, Sea Cat promised himself publicly to right the wrong that had
been done him.

> "I'm going to the dance tonight. I don't know and I don't care
> who's [going to be] there. I'm going to down at least four women
> in the next twenty-four hours."

Thus the men talked of themselves as exploiters and users of
women. But talk is cheap. In practice, in their real relationships
with real women, the men frequently gave the lie to their own
words. For men and women both, naked exploitation, unalloyed
with "liking" or other tempering impulses, was at best a sometime
thing. It occurred most frequently as a kind of upside-down ideal
statement of how one is expected to behave, as lip service to a
public fiction which the individual man or woman is periodically
obliged to acknowledge lest he be ridiculed or dismissed as "lame"
(a weakling, a sucker, a patsy).

The contention that "A man should take anything he can get
when he can get it"; Tally's "Everything New for '62"; Leroy's
"A mule is the best thing to live with"; Sea Cat's announced intention to "down four women"—any four women—in twenty-
four hours were all public expressions of support for the myth or
public fiction of man as the uncompromising exploiter of women.

In action, however, the impulse to use women as objects of
economic or sexual exploitation is deflected by countervailing impulses and goals, especially the desire to build personal, intimate
relationships based on mutual liking or love. It is the interplay of
these opposing impulses which accounts, at least in part, for the
discrepancy between the way men talk about women and the way
they act with them.

Men and women both had to deal with these conflicting impulses and goals. Here, for example, is eighteen-year-old Carol claiming the exploitative ideal for her own and castigating her friend, sixteen-year-old Lena, for making "liking" a precondition for engaging in sex and accepting money from a man. Carol and Lena were unmarried mothers living with their children. This conversation took place on the front steps of the house from which they had just been evicted. Their belongings were piled up on the sidewalk in front of us. I asked Lena whether she was receiving ADC. She said no, she wouldn't have anything like that. On ADC, she said, you can't live your own life.[5] "You can't have any boy friends or nothing, and I sure like my boys."

"You like your boys, all right," said Carol, "but you better start learning to like some of that money, too."

Carol turned to me. "Do you know what she did the other day," she said, indicating Lena with a contemptuous toss of her head. "This man wanted to give her twenty dollars for some pussy and she wouldn't give him any."

"I just didn't like him," said Lena.

"'Like him,' shit," snapped Carol. "I wish he had asked me for some pussy and him with twenty dollars in his pocket."

Like Carol, the men proclaimed themselves uncompromising exploiters; like Lena, they did not always "take what you can get when you can get it." They sometimes turned down women who were available to them and sometimes took the initiative in breaking off relationships from which they benefited economically. Leroy broke off with Louise, "the mule . . . who can really pull

---

5. A reference to Washington's "man-in-the house" rule which excludes women from receiving Aid to Dependent Children if there is an employable male in the household. This grotesque paternalism was enforced by special investigators who made unannounced searches—at all hours of the day and night—for evidence of a "man in the house." Thus were "cheaters" weeded out; that is, undeserving children whose mothers continued to want love or sex even though they had received a check from the Department of Welfare.

that wagon," to return again to Charlene, who was generally judged to be less attractive than Louise and who, instead of supporting Leroy, was almost entirely dependent on him for her own support. Tally, who was fond of assessing women in money terms and who claimed not to understand how Sea Cat could put out a woman when she was working every day, was no better at exploiting economically his own relationships with women than was Sea Cat. Emma Lou had been living with Tally for a few weeks and wanted to go on living with him. Tally wanted her to leave. Emma Lou offered to turn her weekly pay (about forty-five dollars) over to him in its entirety. Tally refused and shortly forced her out, although he had no other regular woman at this time.[6]

Sea Cat was generally acknowledged as one of the most successful lovers and managers of man-woman relationships, yet it is in Sea Cat's relationship with women that the public pose of the cynical user of women gives way most completely to the private realities. Sally, twenty-one, who lived in the room above Sea Cat's in the rooming house, and Louella, about eighteen, who lived across the street, frequently visited Sea Cat's room. Both were clearly available to him, but he discouraged their advances: Sally, because she was too voluble and unpredictable; Louella because he was afraid she couldn't sustain a casual relationship and would "be all over me." Wives or girl friends of his close friends were excluded from his universe of legitimate sex targets. Sea Cat had many times, for example, gone out with Doris, but her subsequent marriage to a friend of his (one of the men on the corner) changed all this. She was, by his own admission, still very attractive to him but Sea Cat stayed away from her until, about a year after her marriage, he learned she was "cutting out" on her husband. Similarly, when a girl who had been going out with his friend Arthur let it be known that she "liked" Sea Cat, he scrupulously kept her at arm's length.

---

6. See pp. 119ff. for a more detailed account of Tally and Emma Lou.

Sea Cat's capacity for self-denial is clearly evident in his relationship with Linda. If his motive was, at bottom, a sexually selfish one, he showed no rancor when the whole thing failed to come off. In April, Sea Cat met and came to like Linda, a twenty-five-year-old waitress. She lived uptown, but after they had known each other two weeks she began coming to his room after work (2 A.M.) and spending the night there.

"We talk for a while and then we go to bed," said Sea Cat. He said they slept naked, being careful never to touch one another. She had had a bad experience with a man, he explained—he didn't know what[7]—and she was afraid of men. She was afraid of him, too, he added, "but she's learning not to be."

When they had spent four nights in this manner—and occasionally she would also drop in to talk before going to work—Sea Cat had still not kissed her or touched her body because "I like her and I don't want to spoil anything." He felt that he was gradually winning her confidence and that "she'll come to me real soon." Two weeks later, however, she had stopped coming to sleep with him after work. They had not had any sex contact and Sea Cat didn't think they ever would, but they were still "good friends."

This is not to suggest, however, that one must wholly discount men's view of themselves as exploiters and users of women. A poor man who can get hold of some money is that much less poor

---

7. Talk about sex practices and sex practices themselves are characterized by fastidiousness and reserve. In ordinary, general conversation, the short, blunt words commonly used to designate coitus and genitalia are used freely and easily. But when the subject is sex, and as the talk narrows down to one's own person or sex partner, the language becomes less direct and descriptive phrases such as "I really laid some pipe last night" tend to replace the more specific, denotative labels for intercourse. In general, there is a kind of looking away from a close-up of the sex act as if it were a Medusa's head which will not tolerate direct observation. Some of the standard institutionalized techniques for dealing with it directly, as through the use of humor or obscenity, are here weak or unused. Dirty jokes are rare; pornographic pictures are conspicuously absent.

for the moment he has it. And in a world where sexual conquest is one of the few ways in which one can prove one's masculinity, the man who does not make capital of his relationship with a woman is that much less a man.

If one looks at the varied man-woman relationships as different accommodations to the desire to exploit, on one hand, and the desire for a love or liking relationship on the other, two basic modes of accommodation emerge: an ideal mode and a real mode. In the ideal mode, seldom if ever realized in practice, only one set of impulses—either the exploitative or the nonexploitative—is operative in any given relationship. In the second or real mode, both sets of impulses are operative in any given relationship.

In the ideal mode, the man divides his universe of women into two discrete parts: those who are "nice,"[8] and those who are "not

---

8. Although being "nice" is perhaps the most desirable quality in a woman, it is a quality that is poorly defined and one that varies according to one or another man's perspective. To say that a woman is nice can, in some contexts, be a specific reference to her sexiness or to some other specific attribute, such as her having a good job or other income. More often, however, when a man says "She's real nice," he means he approves of her as a total person, and "nice" becomes a kind of judgmental distillate of the woman's personal, ethical, social and esthetic qualities.

There is, of course, no absolute consensus on who is or who isn't nice and even one man's opinion may change over time as his knowledge of or relationship with a given woman changes. There are, however, some broad and relatively objective standards which most men would subscribe to. Great importance is attached to a woman's personal appearance and habits. A nice woman does not dress in "raggedy-ass clothes," nor otherwise appear slovenly or unkempt. Her body, her children, if any, and her living quarters are routinely clean and neat in appearance. She is a conscientious wage-earner or homemaker, or both, and not at all like the woman who lounges in a housecoat all day, the bed unmade, the children unwashed and uncombed, and waits for her man to bring her some money or for the mailman to bring her welfare check.

Her ethics bespeak a fundamental honesty and decency. She does not say one thing to your face, another behind your back. She is not sexually promiscuous and while she may not necessarily remain wholly faithful to her husband or boy friend, she "cuts out on him" discreetly, with selected persons, and usually only after provocation, such as mistreatment or repeated and public infidelity on his part. Honesty means simple honesty in the property sense, too. She does not steal.

nice." One part is reserved exclusively for exploitation; to the other part he is prepared to accord more considerate treatment. Sea Cat makes the distinction and claims to act accordingly, as the following incident reveals.

Sea Cat was changing his clothes preparatory to going out. I flopped on his bed to wait for him and a package of prophylactics fell out from under the mattress. In replacing it, I discovered a dozen or more similar packages. I asked Sea Cat if he always used them. He said no, sometimes he does, sometimes he doesn't.

> "It depends on the girl. If she's nice, friendly and all that, the kind I wouldn't mind helping out, then I don't use them. But if she's not nice, I don't take any chances."[9]

It is this ideal division of women into two distinct categories, only one of which is designated for exploitation, which permits the man to enter freely and publicly into the more satisfying give-and-take relationships based on liking or love. By claiming to exploit—or actually exploiting—Sally and Irene, Harry is free to declare his liking or love for Mary without seriously compromising his own or others' image of him as the tough and cynical realist. In this way, romantic love is legitimized in the streetcorner world which pretends to use, as one measure of a man, his willingness

---

In her social relationships a nice woman displays a generosity of spirit; she is friendly, accessible, tolerant, and open and easy of manner. Importantly, whatever her "ways" or style, she is fun to be with.

9. From a middle-class point of view, one would expect the man to protect the "nice" girl against the possibility of conception and to let the "not nice" girl take her chances. Behind this attitude lies the middle-class contempt for the "not nice" (lower-class?) girl who can justly be left to her own devices even if she does conceive. Sea Cat's morality is of a somewhat different order. Acknowledging his responsibility to "help out" any woman whom he gets pregnant, he forestalls having to enter into an ongoing, helping relationship with the "not nice" girl by using contraceptives. There is no such pressing need to use contraceptives with the "nice" girl since he has no strong aversion to the continuing relationship with her that conception would entail.

and ability to take what he can get from women whenever he can get it. Thus, Leroy, having publicly established his support of the myth of exploitation by claiming that "A mule is the best thing to live with," by claiming that Louise pays for everything when they go out and by similar declarations, is free to enter into a mutual love relationship with Charlene with impunity.

Indeed, declarations of romantic love are integral parts of a great many of the man-woman relationships, especially when the relationship has been strained, as after a quarrel, or during the early stages of its growth while enthusiasm still runs high. Here is one of Leroy's letters to Charlene, written about two weeks after their first meeting in the Carry-out shop:

> SWEETHEART, time and opportunity spare me no greater pleasure than to take this leisure time to communicate with you the very thoughts that I have at this instant. However, some people go with you because of your beauty but I like you for your intelligence and the wonderful way you carry yourself. These are the things that upset me. The days that I have may have been wonderful and generous days. That is why I can say that the love I have for you is the greatest love a man could ever have for a woman. With this I bring this letter to an abrupt halt. So until the mailman knocks again, be sweet and remain the wonderful Charlene that I shall always remember. LOVE, LEROY ALLEN BROWN

Ten days later, after a quarrel, he writes again, protesting his desolation and his own unworthiness.

> . . . although we have known each other for a few months [in fact it was weeks, not months], I feel as though those few months with you will always remain a wonderful and admirable remembrance . . . I want to ask you for forgiveness . . . I realized you'll find another young man to fill the emptiness in your heart. I wish the both of you the best of luck because when you were mine I didn't treat you right. Just like a king, I've lost everything. I stood all alone on

my throne . . . I shall always remember you, Charlene. Love, MR.
NOBODY

Leroy was one of the younger men on the corner and by far
the most literate, but gallant declarations of romantic love were
not limited to the young and the verbally artful. Stanton was twice
Leroy's age and illiterate. He was in love with Bernice and also
expressed his feelings in the tradition of courtly love, marking her
as one whom he would not exploit. He took pride in his concern
for her reputation and safety; he declared publicly his love for her
and took a public oath to "treat her right," which included,
among other things, a willingness to be on the giving rather than
the taking end of their relationship.

Bernice was going to leave Edward, said Stanton. The day before, Edward and Bernice had a fight and Edward took back the
watch he had given her. Stanton said that this was a stupid thing
for Edward to do. Edward just didn't know how to treat Bernice.

> She's not going to stay with him anymore. She's coming over
> to [live with] me and man, I sure do love that woman! I'm going
> to treat her right, too. When I give her something, it's hers, and I'll
> never take it back.

This idealized mode of man-woman relationships in which
there is a clear division between exploitation and nonexploitation
is more a wish than a fact. Only exceptionally does this clear division work out in practice for it is very difficult to keep a given
relationship at all times from spilling over the dividing line. The
result is that most man-woman relationships fall into the second
mode in which both the exploitative and nonexploitative (e.g.,
"liking") impulses are operative in the same relationships (as they
were, in fact, in Leroy's relationships with Louise and Charlene
and in Stanton's relationship with Bernice). In this second mode,
the man tends to have mixed feelings about the relationship. His

attitude and behavior toward the woman tend to appear inconsistent and even contradictory as now one, now the other, impulse takes over. Sea Cat and Gloria are a good example.

Sea Cat's relationship with Gloria was a public affair. The men on the corner, like the chorus in a Greek tragedy, watched its development, analyzed it, and commented on it. They saw—or talked as if they saw—Sea Cat and Gloria as the user and the used, with Sea Cat a kind of Streetcorner Everyman who hunts for A Good Thing, finds it, and inevitably loses it. Sea Cat carefully fostered this image of himself and Gloria.

Sea Cat met Gloria in July 1962 at a recreation and amusement center in nearby Maryland. Gloria liked Sea Cat and they started going out together. Gloria was a short, stocky, pleasant-faced widow of twenty-five. Her husband had died the year before and Gloria, who was the beneficiary of his life insurance, also inherited his one-half interest in several modest but profitable commercial enterprises. She owned two cars and a beach cottage in Maryland.

Two weeks after their first meeting, Sea Cat and Gloria had become close friends. They had gone to several parties together and spent a Sunday at her beach cottage. Gloria gave Sea Cat the use of her Bonneville convertible. Sea Cat announced—and all the men on the corner agreed—that he "had it made." Sea Cat made no secret of the fact that Gloria was calling the shots in this relationship. He explained that "this [relationship] is a big thing" for him and he didn't want to jeopardize it in any way. He said he was leaving the initiative entirely with her.

As the summer wore on, he and Gloria grew closer together and Sea Cat appeared less and less frequently on the corner. Once, Gloria came to the Carry-out shop with Sea Cat, and once or twice Stanton or one of the other men went along with them to her house or to the beach cottage for a day. But in the main, Sea Cat was drawn into her social circle and maintained only sporadic contact with the Carry-out.

By the end of the year, Sea Cat had moved into a modest but

new apartment about five blocks away from the Carry-out. Gloria furnished it and paid the rent. In February of the following year, Sea Cat's oldest child died. His wife and children, together with her parents, had moved to Detroit. Gloria gave Sea Cat the money to go there and to contribute to the funeral expenses.

According to Sea Cat, when he made one of his infrequent appearances on the corner, all was well. But in March and April there were rumors that he was "messing up." Richard said he had seen Sea Cat at the Checkerboard Lounge with another woman. Stanton said that he had heard that Sea Cat had wrecked Gloria's car while riding with another woman and that "Gloria's getting tired of his shit." The men on the corner shook their heads. Some said that Sea Cat couldn't stay away from all those women. Others said that he was a damn fool for letting women "come between him and A Good Thing." In May, Gloria called a halt. She took back her car and Sea Cat was forced to give up the apartment and the furniture. When the men on the corner learned about this, they shrugged their shoulders. "I knew it was coming," some of them said. "It had to happen," said the others.

A short time later Sea Cat appeared at a Saturday night party given by one of the men on the corner. His reserve and self-depre-cation were conspicuous among the laughter and shouting of drinking and good fellowship. When he spoke at all, he spoke in a low, quiet voice.

> I had it made but I blew it. I blew it. I really loved that woman. She gave me everything she had. Not the money, I don't mean that. She used to say that when a woman gave a man her body she was giving him everything that a woman had to give. I really loved her, and she loved me too.

For the next few weeks, Sea Cat had difficulty in pulling him-self together. Gloria finally agreed to his desperate pleas for another meeting, one in which he hoped to effect a reconciliation, but Sea

Cat, now the hurt and unrequited lover, spoiled it all by slapping her for reasons which he did not understand himself, either at the time or in retrospect. Now, it was over between them. And it was clear to everyone that, however opportunistically Sea Cat had manipulated the relationship in its beginning, the end of it found him mourning his loss more in emotional than in money terms. He had been as much the lover as the user, maybe more.

6

FRIENDS AND NETWORKS

More than most social worlds, perhaps, the streetcorner world takes its shape and color from the structure and character of the face-to-face relationships of the people who live in it. Unlike other areas in our society, where a large portion of the individual's energies, concerns and time are invested in self-improvement, career and job development, family and community activities, religious and cultural pursuits, or even in broad, impersonal social and political issues, these resources in the streetcorner world are almost entirely given over to the construction and maintenance of personal relationships.

On the streetcorner, each man has his own network of these personal relationships and each man's network defines for him the members of his personal community.[1] His personal community, then, is not a bounded area but rather a web-like arrangement of man-man and man-woman relationships in which he is selectively attached in a particular way to a definite number of discrete per-

---

1. I have borrowed this term from Jules Henry and taken the liberty of defining it differently and limiting its scope (to exclude, for example, from a man's personal community, his employer, the policeman on the beat, or other agents of local, state and national governments whom he may look to for support). See "The Personal Community and Its Invariant Properties."

sons. In like fashion, each of these persons has his own personal network.[2]

At the edges of this network are those persons with whom his relationship is affectively neutral, such as area residents whom he has "seen around" but does not know except to nod or say "hi" to as they pass on the street. These relationships are limited to simple recognition. Also at the edges are those men and women, including former friends and acquaintances, whom he dislikes or fears or who dislike or fear him. These relationships are frequently characterized by avoidance but the incumbents remain highly visible and relevant to one another.

In toward the center are those persons he knows and likes best, those with whom he is "up tight": his "walking buddies," "good" or "best" friends, girl friends, and sometimes real or putative kinsmen. These are the people with whom he is in more or less daily, face-to-face contact, and whom he turns to for emergency aid, comfort or support in time of need or crisis. He gives them and receives from them goods and services in the name of friendship, ostensibly keeping no reckoning. Routinely, he seeks them out and is sought out by them. They serve his need to be with others of his kind, and to be recognized as a discrete, distinctive personality, and he, in turn, serves them the same way. They are both his audience and his fellow actors.

It is with these men and women that he spends his waking, nonworking hours, drinking, dancing, engaging in sex, playing the fool or the wise man, passing the time at the Carry-out or on the streetcorner, talking about nothing and everything, about epistemology or Cassius Clay, about the nature of numbers or how he would "have it made" if he could have a steady job that paid him $60 a week with no layoffs.

---

2. "A network is a social configuration in which some, but not all, of the component external units maintain relationships with one another. The external units do not make up a larger social whole. They are not surrounded by a common boundary." Elizabeth Bott, *Family and Social Network*, pp. 216–217.

So important a part of daily life are these relationships that it seems like no life at all without them. Old Mr. Jenkins climbed out of his sickbed to take up a seat on the Coca-Cola case at the Carry-out for a couple of hours. "I can't stay home and play dead," he explained, "I got to get out and see my friends."

Friendship is sometimes anchored in kinship, sometimes in long-term associations which may reach back into childhood. Other close friendships are born locally, in the streetcorner world itself, rather than brought in by men from the outside. Such friendships are built on neighbor or co-worker relationships, or on a shared experience or other event or situation which brings two people together in a special way.

In general, close friendships tend to develop out of associations with those who are already in one's network of personal relationships: relatives, men and women who live in the area and spend much of their time on the street or in public places, and co workers. The result is that the streetcorner man, perhaps more than others in our society, tends to use the same individuals over and over again: he may make a friend, neighbor and co-worker of his kinsman, or a friend, co-worker and kinsman of his neighbor. A look at some of the personal relationships can illustrate the many-stranded aspects of friendship and the bi-directional character of friendship on the one hand, and kinship, neighbor, co-worker and other relationships on the other.

When Tonk and Pearl got married and took an apartment near the Carry-out, Pearl's brother, Boley, moved in with them. Later, Pearl's nephew, J.R., came up from their hometown in North Carolina and he, too, moved in with them. J.R. joined Tonk and Boley on the streetcorner and when Earl told Tonk of some job openings where he worked, Tonk took J.R. with him. These three, then, were kinsmen, shared the same residence, hung out together on the streetcorner, and two of them—for a time at least—were co-workers.

Preston was Clarence's uncle. They lived within a block of

each other and within two blocks of the Carry-out. Clarence worked on a construction job and later got Preston a job at the same place. Tally, Wee Tom and Budder also worked at the same construction site. The five men regularly walked back from the job to the streetcorner together, usually sharing a bottle along the way. On Friday afternoons, they continued drinking together for an hour or so after returning to the streetcorner. Tally referred to the other four men as his "drinking buddies."

Tally had met Wee Tom on the job. Through Tally, Wee Tom joined them on the walk home, began to hang around the Carry-out and finally moved into the neighborhood as well. Budder had been the last to join the group at the construction site. He had known Preston and Clarence all along, but not well. He first knew Tally as a neighbor. They came to be friends through Tally's visits to the girl who lived with Budder, his common-law wife, and his wife's children. When Tally took Budder onto the job with him, Budder became a co-worker and drinking buddy, too. Thus, in Tally's network, Wee Tom began as co-worker, moved up to drinking buddy, neighbor and finally close friend; Budder from neighbor and friend to co-worker. Importantly, and irrespective of the direction in which the relationships developed, the confluence of the co-worker and especially the neighbor relationship with friendship deepened the friend relationship.

One of the most striking aspects of these overlapping relationships is the use of kinship as a model for the friend relationship. Most of the men and women on the streetcorner are unrelated to one another and only a few have kinsmen in the immediate area. Nevertheless, kinship ties are frequently manufactured to explain, account for, or even to validate friend relationships. In this manner, one could move from friendship to kinship in either direction. One could start with kinship, say, as did Preston and Clarence or Boley and Tonk and build on this, or conversely, one could start with friendship and build a kin relationship.

The most common form of the pseudo-kin relationship between two men is known as "going for brothers." This means, simply, that two men agree to present themselves as brothers to the outside world and to deal with one another on the same basis. Going for brothers appears as a special case of friendship in which the usual claims, obligations, expectations, and loyalties of the friend relationship are publicly declared to be at their maximum.

Sea Cat and Arthur went for brothers. Sea Cat's room was Arthur's home so far as he had one anywhere. It was there that he kept his few clothes and other belongings, and it was on Sea Cat's dresser that he placed the pictures of his girl friends (sent "with love" or "love and kisses"). Sea Cat and Arthur wore one another's clothes and, whenever possible or practical, were in one another's company. Even when not together, each usually had a good idea of where the other was or had been or when he would return. Generally, they seemed to prefer going with women who were themselves friends; for a period of a month or so, they went out with two sisters.

Sea Cat worked regularly; Arthur only sporadically or for long periods not at all. His own credit of little value, Arthur sometimes tried to borrow money from the men on the corner, saying that the lender could look to his "brother" for payment. And when Sea Cat found a "good thing" in Gloria, who set him up with a car and his own apartment,[3] Arthur shared in his friend's good fortune. On the streetcorner or in Sea Cat's room, they laughed and horsed around together, obviously enjoying one another's company. They cursed each other and called each other names in mock anger or battle, taking liberties that were reserved for and tolerated in close friends alone.[4]

---

3. See pp. 102ff.

4. Once, in his room, Sea Cat complained that a can of hair spray cost him more than $3.00, but that, with Arthur around, a can didn't even last a week. Arthur seemed not to have heard. Slowly, he got up from the bed, took a can of hair spray from the dresser, ostentatiously loosened his belt, pulled his pants away from his waist and with great deliberation sprayed his genitals, looking at Sea Cat with an air of

A few of the men on the corner knew that Sea Cat and Arthur were, in fact, unrelated. A few knew they were not brothers but thought they were probably related in some way. Others took their claim to kinship at face value. Even those who knew they were merely going for brothers, however, accepted this as evidence of the special character of their friend relationship. In general, only those who are among the most important in one's personal network can distinguish between real and pseudo-kin relationships, partly because the question as to whether two men are really brothers or are simply going for brothers is not especially relevant. The important thing for people to know in their interaction with the two men is that they say they are brothers, not whether they are or not.

The social reality of the pseudo-kinship tie between those who are "going for brothers" is clearly evident in the case of Richard and Leroy. Richard and Leroy had been going for brothers for three months or so when Leroy got in a fight with a group of teenagers and young adults. Leroy suffered serious internal injuries and was hospitalized for more than a month. One week after the fight, Richard and one of the teenagers who had beaten up Leroy, and with whom both he and Leroy had been on friendly terms, got into a fight over a private matter having nothing to do with Leroy, and Richard killed the teenager. Richard was immediately arrested and the police, acting on information from the dead boy's friends, relatives, and others in the community, charged him with first degree murder for the premeditated revenge killing of one who had beaten up "his brother." But when it was established that Leroy and Richard were not related in any way the charge was dropped to murder in the second degree. The dead boy's friends and relatives were outraged and bewildered. To them, and even to some of Richard and Leroy's friends, it was clearly a pre-

---

blank innocence all the while. Sea Cat shook his head. "See what I mean?" he said, but he couldn't quite suppress his laughter.

meditated, deliberate killing. Hadn't Richard and Leroy been going for brothers? And hadn't Leroy been badly beaten by this same boy just eight days earlier?

Pseudo-kinship ties are also invoked in certain man-woman relationships. Stoopy first met Lucille in the kitchen of an officers' club in Virginia where they both worked. They became friends and later, when Lucille and her teen-age son were looking for a place to live, Stoopy told her of a place in the Carry-out area and Lucille moved in. As neighbors as well as co-workers, Stoopy and Lucille's friendship deepened and they "went for cousins." Stoopy and Lucille saw a lot of one another. They frequently went back and forth to work together. They borrowed money from each other and freely visited each other in their homes. Lucille came to know Stoopy's wife through her Saturday morning visits with the children, and Stoopy's relationship with Lucille's son was conspicuously warm and avuncular.[5]

At no time in their relationship was there ever the slightest suggestion of any romantic or sexual connection between them. Indeed, this seems to be the primary purpose behind "going for cousins." It is a way of saying, "This woman [man] and I are good friends but we are not lovers." Given the taboo against cousin marriage,[6] going for cousins permits an unrelated man and woman to enter into a close-friend relationship without compromising their romantic or sexual status in any way. It is a public disclaimer

---

5. Later, after Lucille moved out, she sometimes visited Stoopy and others in the Carry-out area (see p. 127). During this period, she and Stoopy continued to go for cousins.

6. The aura of incest associated with sex relationships between (first) cousins may explain the following episode. In this particular case, even a sexual relationship with one's cousin's spouse appears as an unthinkable proposition. Wee Tom and I had been in Nancy's place. Among the others there, were a man and woman neither of us knew. Later the same evening we met them again on a streetcorner. The man went into a drugstore. The woman tried to kiss me and I pushed her away. "What do you want with him? You already got your man," said Wee Tom, pointing to the man in the drug store. "Him?" she said, indignantly. "He's married to my cousin. How could he be my man?"

of any romantic or sexual content in a cross-sex, close-friend relationship.

The social utility of going for cousins is evident when one compares Stoopy and Lucille with Tally and Velma. Tally and Velma were good friends, but unlike Stoopy and Lucille, they were not going for cousins.[7] On several occasions Tally and Velma attended parties as part of a foursome, each bringing his own partner. On such occasions, Tally often spoke of his friendship with Velma, noting that he had several times slept in her home but had "never laid a hand on her." Skeptical or even uninterested listeners were dragged before Velma who verified Tally's description of their relationship.

In contrast, Stoopy and Lucille were under no such pressure to validate the asexual nature of their relationship. The question never came up. They were going for cousins. That was enough.

Sometimes pseudo-kinship is invoked in more casual terms, apparently to sharpen and lend formal structure to a relationship which is generally vague. Occasionally, one hears that "he just call her his sister," or that "they just call it brother and sister" or even "they just go for brother and sister." Such was the case with Stanton. His young daughter was living with a married woman whom most people, including Stanton, referred to as his sister. But Stanton, "he just call her his sister." In caring for his child, the woman was, of course, doing what sisters sometimes do. The assignment of the label "sister" to one already performing a function which frequently appears in association with that label was an easy step to take. A vague relationship was rendered specific; it was simplified, and the need for explanations was reduced. This may also have

---

7. I do not know why Tally and Velma did not go for cousins. Perhaps they did not see enough of each other (Velma lived across the river in Virginia) to warrant taking this step. Perhaps they were not prepared to commit themselves to the obligations that such a formalization of their relationship would entail. Perhaps they did not want to preclude the possibility that their relationship might develop along romantic lines. Or finally, perhaps they were beginning the process of going for cousins.

served to discourage public suspicion about the nature of this relationship. In these respects, perhaps going for cousins would have served them equally well. And as in the case of going for brothers, whether Stanton and this woman were in fact brother and sister was less important than the fact that they "called" themselves so. The woman's husband, we must assume, knew they were not related. But since Stanton and the man's wife called themselves brother and sister, the husband's vested interests and public status were not jeopardized, not even by Stanton's visits to his home when he himself was not present.

Most friendships are thus born in propinquity, in relationships or situations in which individuals confront one another day by day and face to face. These friendships are nurtured and supported by an exchange of money, goods, services and emotional support. Small loans, ranging from a few pennies up to two or three dollars, are constantly being asked for and extended. Leroy watches Malvina's children while she goes out to have a few drinks with a friend. Tonk and Stanton help Budder move the old refrigerator he just bought into his apartment. Robert spends an evening giving Richard a home process. Preston lends Stoopy forty cents for bus fare to go to work. Pearl and Tonk throw a party, supplying all of the food and much of the liquor themselves. When Bernice leaves Stanton, Leroy consoles him telling him of how Charlene is always doing this too, but always coming back. Leroy borrows a bottle of milk for the baby from Richard and Shirley. Sara gives Earl three dollars to get his clothes out of the cleaners. Sea Cat and Stoopy find Sweets knocked unconscious on the sidewalk, carry him home and put him to bed. Tonk and Richard go down to the police station to put up five dollars toward Tally's collateral. Clarence returns from his father's funeral where Tally and Preston hung onto him throughout, restraining him physically where necessary and comforting him in his shock as best they could. Back at Nancy's place, Clarence nurses his grief in silence and nonparticipation. Tally urges him again and again to "Come on, Baby, show me you're a man," but Clarence shakes his head no. Tally keeps trying. Finally, taking the glass of whiskey offered him, Clarence sloughs off his mourner's status by dancing with Nancy. Tally laughs with pleasure at his own handiwork. "O.K. now?" he asks, and Clarence smiles back that yes, everything's O.K. now.

In ways such as these, each person plays an important part in helping and being helped by those in his personal network. Since much of the cooperation between friends centers around the basic prerequisites of daily living, friends are of special importance to one's sense of physical and emotional security. The more friends one has or believes himself to have, and the deeper he holds these friendships to be, the greater his self-esteem and the greater the esteem for himself he thinks he sees in the eyes of others.

The pursuit of security and self-esteem push him to romanticize his perception of his friends and friendships. He wants to see acquaintances as friends, and not only as friends but as friends with whom he is "up tight," "walking buddies," "best friends," or even brothers. He prefers to see the movement of money, goods, services and emotional support between friends as flowing freely out of loyalty and generosity and according to need rather than as a mutual exchange resting securely on a quid pro quo basis. He wants to believe that his friendships reach back into the distant past and have an unlimited future; that he knows and is known by his friends intimately, that they can trust one another implicitly, and that their loyalties to one another are almost unbounded. He wants to see himself as Pythias to other Damons.

"Wee Tom's my best friend," said Tally, two months after they first met. He put his hand on Wee Tom's shoulder. "Him and me are up tight. Nothing I have is too good for him." Wee Tom said the same went for him.

When Arthur was shot to death by the shopkeeper whom he was trying to hold up, Richard said that the shopkeeper had, in effect, killed himself as well as killed Arthur. Arthur was his— Richard's—friend and neither he nor Arthur's other friends would let their buddy's death go unavenged. When Shirley protested that the man killed Arthur in self-defense, that Arthur was in the wrong, and what about the consequences of revenge to Richard, herself and the children, Richard dismissed her with a shrug. "I can't break it down for you. You just don't understand [how it is between friends]."

Leroy said he and all the roomers in the house didn't pay Malvina any fixed amount of rent. Everybody just gave what they could when they could. They were all friends, you know, and it was oh, so informal: from each according to his ability, to each according to his need.

But Tally and Wee Tom did have things that were "too good" for each other, and their friendship was gradually eroded by arguments over money[8] and a variety of other things, including the relative priority of friendship claims against those of the husband-wife relationship.[9]

And Richard, who did not go to Arthur's funeral,[10] never again mentioned avenging his friend's death, even when the subject of Arthur came up.

As for Leroy's contention that Malvina and the others he was living with at the time were one big family, sharing one hearth, one pot, the fact is that each person or couple purchased their own

---

8. Such as the time Tally hit the number for a quarter ($135.00) and not only refused to give Wee Tom $5 or $10 (which Wee Tom didn't really expect) but also refused to lend him more than $5.00.

9. Wee Tom and I were in Tally's room, waiting for Tally to finish dressing. As Tally peeled off his undershirt, he began berating Wee Tom for leaving him and the others after they got paid. Wee Tom protested that "You can't always do what you want to do. Sometimes you do what you gotta do, and I had to get home. My old lady needed the money to pay the rent and we had a lot to talk about. That don't mean we're not friends. I just had to go home, that was all." Tally sneered at this. "A woman's got to come up to a man," he answered. "If a woman don't come up to me, fuck her. Throw her ass out." Wee Tom was annoyed and angry but he said nothing.

10. He later gave as his reason the fact that he did not have the money to get his hair fixed.

food and kept it under lock and key in one of the four refrigerators in the kitchen in the basement. Everyone had the right to use the toilet on the second floor, the kitchen, and the handful of pots, pans and dishes lying dirty in the sink or on the drainboard, but nothing else was held in common. Moreover, careful mental accounts were kept, not only of rent, but of less formal exchanges as well, nor were the figures rounded off. Here is Leroy reconstructing on tape the events leading up to his last break with Malvina and others in the house.[11] Charlene had told Leroy that Malvina said she wanted the money he owed her for rent and other expenses:

> So when I got paid I went down there. I said, "Malvina, here is your twelve ninety-five . . . ." I said, "Now, I want a dollar and a half from you for your haircut; I want two dollars for the money I gave you to buy the liquor and I want a dollar and seventy-five cents for the money you got the other day." Then I said, "Malvina, I want five dollars from you from where I got the groceries and I want the four dollars that you got then."
>
> [Caricaturing Malvina] "Well, I ain't got it right now."
>
> I said, "Then I'll wait until you get paid. When you all get paid I'm gonna come down here and I'm gonna have my list ready. When we get to five dollars, you subtract that money from what you all owe me and have my money ready."
>
> So when they got the money, they said, "We got to pay the rent."
>
> I said, "I don't know nothing about that. My rent's paid. All I wants is my money. If I don't get my money, you can take that on my rent. I ain't paying the rent for the next three weeks."
>
> So I didn't pay no rent for the next three weeks. We kept on arguing. Then last night, Malvina jumped up . . .

Friendship is at its romantic, flamboyant best when things are going well for the persons involved. But friendship does not often

---

11. "It's only when the relationship breaks down that the underlying obligations are brought to light." William Foote Whyte, *Street Corner Society*, p. 257.

stand up well to the stress of crisis or conflict of interest, when demands tend to be heaviest and most insistent. Everyone knows this. Extravagant pledges of aid and comfort between friends are, at one level, made and received in good faith. But at another level, fully aware of his friends' limited resources and the demands of their self-interest, each person is ultimately prepared to look to himself alone.

The recognition that, at bottom, friendship is not a bigger-than-life relationship is sometimes expressed as a repudiation of all would-be friends ("I don't need you or any other mother-fucker") or as a cynical denial that friendship as a system of mutual aid and support exists at all. When Tally threatened to withdraw his friendship from Richard, Richard dismissed this as no real loss. "Richard's the only one who ever looked out for Richard," he said.[12]

A similar attitude leads to the assessment of friendship as a "fair weather" phenomenon. John had just been fired from his job. Bernice, Betty and I were speculating about the reason for it. I told them what I had heard on the corner.

> "I know who told you that, but they all talk about John behind his back," said Bernice.
> I said that the person who told me what I had repeated to them considered himself John's friend.
> "He ain't no friend of John's. He never was," retorted Bernice. "I know who told you and I know he's not John's friend."
> Betty said, "None of them's John's friend. All those boys—Sea Cat, Richard, Tally, Leroy—they're the ones cost John his job. They're not his friends. You know, when a person's up, the whole world's up with him. But when a person's down, you're down alone."

Attitudes toward friends and friendships are thus always shifting, frequently ambivalent, and sometimes contradictory. One

---

12. See p. 120 for the context of this assertion.

moment, friendship is an almost sacred covenant; the next, it is the locus of cynical exploitation: "Friends are [good only] for money."

These shifts and apparent contradictions arise directly out of the structure and character of the individual's network of personal relationships. They arise from the fact that, at any given moment, the different relationships that comprise the individual's network of personal relationships may be at widely different stages of development or degeneration. They arise, too, from the easy quickness with which a casual encounter can ripen into an intense man–man or man–woman relationship, and the equal ease with which these relationships break down under stress.

One gains a feeling for the fluidity and processual character of personal relations and their networks by looking at one such network over time. The following accounts have been selected from Tally's network of personal relationships for the eight-month period ending August 1962, when he moved out of the Carry-out shop area.[13]

Tally and Richard—In March 1962 Tally was "up tight" (bosom buddies) with Richard. They idled together in and around the Carry-out shop and occasionally spent time together in the basement apartment where Richard lived with his wife Shirley and their three children.

Richard worked hard as a janitor and odd-jobs man, but was chronically short of cash. Tally regularly lent Richard two to five dollars a week on Wednesdays and Richard regularly paid him back on Fridays. At the end of March, Tally offered to take Richard to his own job where they had an opening for laborers, but Richard decided to remain with his janitor's job.

Early in May, Tally happened to be in Richard's apartment

---

13. Tally had moved into the Carry-out area in November 1961. He had been unemployed for most of the winter of 1961–1962. In late February he landed a job on a downtown construction project.

when Shirley's cousin, Emma Lou, arrived unannounced from New York to live with Shirley and Richard while she tried her luck in Washington. The next day, Tally and Emma Lou became lovers. Tally began to visit Richard's apartment freely and sometimes spent the night, sleeping with Emma Lou in the living room. Richard and Tally grew even closer together. Tally told Richard that if anything ever happened to Richard he wouldn't have to worry about his wife and children because he, Tally, would see that they were cared for. Richard said that Tally was one of his best friends.

Two weeks after Emma Lou's arrival, Richard was given the choice of giving up his apartment and his janitor's job or taking a fifty percent cut in pay. The next night, openly worried about the choices confronting him and chafing because, under his wife's surveillance, he was unable to sneak off to meet a girl friend, Richard got drunk on a half-pint of Old Forester and manufactured an incident. He accused his wife Shirley of "liking" and "going out" with Tally and, announcing his determination to "put her out," marched off down the street. Tally followed Richard to "straighten him out." When Tally caught up with Richard about two blocks away, Richard pulled a kitchen knife out of his belt. Tally stopped short.

"Don't stop, you mother, don't stop," Richard shouted, and beckoned with his knife, daring Tally to approach him. Richard said he was "not going to take any more shit" from Tally, and Tally suggested that he put away the knife and fight "man to man." Richard, about as tall as Tally but weighing some fifty pounds less, ridiculed this and they briefly argued the merits of Tally's suggestion.

Then Richard charged Tally with going out with Shirley, adding that he had known all along that Tally wanted her; that he as much as said so last week (referring to Tally's vow to care for Richard's family if anything happened to Richard).

"You wanted me out of the way so that you could have

them," said Richard. "Okay, I'm finished with them, you take 'em."

Tally stamped his foot in disgust. "You know what I meant," he said. "I said that because you and me was up tight. You was one of my best friends, and I don't go out with a friend's wife."

Richard called Tally a liar and offered a list of names of women as evidence. "And what the hell do you do in 203 and 417 [apartments in Richard's building]? You and John were up tight and you're up tight with Flora's old man, too, but that don't stop you from knocking off Flora every night." Ignoring all but the final reference, Tally protested that "I didn't even know Flora's husband's name. You call that 'up tight'?"

They argued this point to a standoff and finally Tally walked off, saying that Richard was drunk and couldn't be talked to. Richard returned to the streetcorner of his apartment house. His wife and her cousin were there. Shirley was crying hard.

Richard said, "Tomorrow I'm going to Baltimore. Washington doesn't owe me anything—not money or anything else. Just a little fun."

"What about me?" cried Shirley. "What about me and the children?"

"Tally likes you so much he can have you," said Richard. "He said he'll take care of you and the kids."

Shirley buried her face in her hands. Emma Lou put her arms around Shirley's shoulders and herded her back into the apartment house. Tally approached Richard again a few minutes later. With measured earnestness Tally told Richard that he had lost a friend and that things would never be the same again between them no matter what happened. Richard said that Tally was wrong; that he, Richard, was twenty-three years old and had never had a friend in his life; that Richard had always been the only one who looked out for Richard and always would be. Tally reminded Richard of all the times he had lent Richard money. Richard said he always paid him back and demanded to know if he owed Tally anything.

"Yes," said Tally. "You remember, you owe me a dollar from last week when you wanted to get back in that crap game."

Richard told Tally not to go away. He ran inside and came back out with a dollar bill and threw it at Tally.

"Now we're even," he said. "I don't owe you nothin' and you don't owe me nothin'. And Tally, I want to tell you one thing: don't ever step across my door again. If you ever put one foot in my house Tally, I'll kill you, I swear to God."

"And Jackson," Richard continued, taking out his knife again and waving it in Tally's face, "don't ever think you're going to catch me without this. From now on whenever you see me, daytime, nighttime, or any other time, I'm always going to have somethin' on me."

Despite the knife, Tally stayed within arm's length. "Richard, I ain't afraid of you and I ain't afraid of your knife. But I ain't mad at you, Richard, so I don't want to fight you. But don't make me mad."

"Get mad then," said Richard. "I'm mad. You get mad, too, and let's have it out." Richard said that he wasn't afraid of the police, that he had been in jail before and had gotten out and if he was in again he'd get out again.

"Maybe you would," said Tally, "but you'd have to go out and scuffle to get them dollars." Tally slapped his back pockets with both hands. "But not me," he said. "I always carry that stuff with me. I always got some right here. I don't have to scuffle for mine. I always got it."

Richard mumbled something weakly and unintelligibly. He was hurt. I tugged at Tally's arm and he let me pull him away from the corner. As we walked away Richard's shouts followed us. "You're yellow, Jackson, you're yellow. You're a yellow black mother."

Over a beer in a nearby bar, Tally said he didn't care whether Richard was drunk or not; that he was holding Richard responsible for what he had said and that he and Richard were never going to be friends again.

An hour later, having thrown Shirley and Emma Lou out, Richard was sitting in his apartment. Shirley, still distraught, returned and stood in the doorway, testing his temper. Richard's rage had subsided and he ignored her. This emboldened Shirley and she stepped all the way into the room.

"Where can I go?" she sobbed. "You know I'm all alone, so where can I go? Nobody wants a woman and three babies."

"You can go to Tally Jackson," said Richard. "He wants to take care of you."

"Tally Jackson, Tally Jackson, you and your Tally Jackson," she shouted. "Tally Jackson was your friend, not mine. You're the one who brought him here. You're the one who made him act like this was his home, his kitchen, his food. You're the one who let him come here drunk and sleep here all night. I've never gone around with Tally Jackson and you know it. I was nice to him because he was your friend. I didn't even know his last name until last week."[14]

In the days and months that followed, Tally and Richard ignored each other as best they could. When both happened to be in the Carry-out shop or idling on the street outside, they appeared to take no notice of the other, but neither of them seemed to go out of his way to avoid such meetings. About two weeks or so after the fight Tally told me he would be willing to meet Richard halfway but only if Richard would initiate the reconciliation. I passed this information on to Richard, but he said simply that he was satisfied with the way things were, and that's the way they remained.

Tally and Emma Lou—Emma Lou was twenty-five years old. She and her cousin Shirley had been raised together by Emma Lou's

---

14. Knowledge of last names is a fairly common measure of social distance. See note 22, p. 132.

mother in Woodston, the same small southern town where Richard had grown up. In May, when Emma Lou came down from New York and moved in with Richard and Shirley, Emma Lou had long been separated from her husband. He was living in Washington; their two children were living in Woodston, one with Emma Lou's mother, one with her husband's mother. Emma Lou's third child, fathered by another man, was also living with her mother in Woodston.

Emma Lou was openly allied with Tally and Shirley in the fight with Richard. When Richard threw her and Shirley out of the apartment, she and Richard stood across the street from each other, shouting curses and threats to kill. Richard returned to the apartment, piled her belongings into her suitcase and put it outside the door. Emma Lou, afraid to return while Richard was there, spent the night with Tally in his room. The next day, when Richard went to work, she picked up her suitcase and moved into Tally's room in Miss Carrie's apartment.

Tally understood this to be a temporary arrangement but Emma Lou fought to stay on and refused to look for another place to live. She continued to work as a waitress at a nearby beer joint and offered to turn her wages over to Tally and live with him on a permanent basis. Tally refused and insisted that she look for another place to live. During the third week of her stay, Emma Lou was still spending all of her nonworking hours in their room and Tally was making a point of being out when she came home. Emma Lou spent much of her time at the window calling out to those on the street to ask if they knew where Tally was, or if Tally was idling on the street, asking him to please come up. Occasionally, with obvious annoyance, Tally went upstairs for a few minutes and quickly returned. More often he simply ignored Emma Lou until she tired of calling him and left the window.

On a Friday night, in the fourth week after Emma Lou had moved in with Tally, he put Emma Lou out of his room because he said he found out that she was sleeping with Bobby John. He said he wouldn't have minded if she had been sleeping around with guys he didn't know, but Bobby John was a friend of his and he wasn't going to stand for that stuff. So Emma Lou moved out of Tally's room but remained in the same apartment, sleeping in the living room and becoming a roomer in her own right in Miss Carrie's place. Emma Lou felt she had been treated unfairly and noted with bitterness that while she had lived with Tally he had several times brought women up to their room, but she had never so much as looked at another man.

Once Emma Lou had moved out of his room, Tally was never heard to mention her name again. They were together once more, ten days after Emma Lou had moved out of Tally's room. It was a Sunday afternoon. Tally and Emma Lou were among the ten or twelve men and women dancing and drinking in Miss Carrie's place. Everyone seemed to be having a good time, but Tally and Emma Lou conspicuously avoided dancing with each other and took no notice of the other's presence. About a week later Emma Lou moved out, a bare six weeks since she had first come to stay with Richard and Shirley. No one knew where she had gone.

Tally and Lonny—Lonny was twenty-six years old. He had completed the tenth grade in Washington where he had been raised from infancy by adoptive parents. He had worked at odd jobs such as day laborer and stock clerk before coming to the Carry-out neighborhood.

Tally had first met Lonny in the summer of 1960 when Lonny moved into an area where Tally was then living. About two weeks after their first meeting, Lonny, who had been living with his wife and her mother, was driven out of the apartment by his mother-in-law.[15] Lonny moved in with Tally. He moved out about three

---

15. Tally and several others who knew the situation said that the heart of the problem lay in the fact that Lonny's mother-in-law felt that Lonny was too dark-skinned for her daughter.

weeks later when his wife and mother-in-law moved to another part of town. He and Tally lost touch with one another.

In February 1962 Tally was subpoenaed as a character witness on Lonny's behalf. Lonny was being tried for the strangulation murder of his young wife. On the way to the courthouse, Tally talked about his previous relationship with Lonny and what little he knew about what had been happening to him. "Lonny is a nice guy," Tally concluded with feeling. "He's one hundred percent."

Lonny was found not guilty of intentionally killing his wife but was immediately rearrested (in the courthouse) for violation of probation on an earlier grand larceny charge. Tally played an important role in gaining Lonny's release. He put up five dollars toward the bondsman's fee, helped raise the other thirty-five from Lonny's family, and agreed to cosign a note for the face value of the bond, which the bondsman had insisted on in addition to his fee.

Lonny was finally released on probation for two more years. On the day of his release Tally, Lonny and I had agreed to meet at the corner when Tally got off from work. Lonny had already lined up a temporary job in a hotel kitchen and he was to start that night. Tally was exuberant and we spent most of the evening on the corner celebrating Lonny's release, with Tally roaring with laughter at his friend's good fortune and slapping Lonny on the back as he recounted in detail the events leading up to this moment of reunion and triumph. That day in March was the high point of their relationship.

Lonny, who lived out of the area and worked nights, came to the Carry-out shop area only infrequently. Two months later, however, he changed to a daytime job and regularly came to the Carry-out shop in the evenings after work, quickly picking up with a girl there and several of the men as well.

One evening Tally asked Lonny for the five dollars he had put up toward Lonny's bond. Lonny shrugged his shoulders and walked away. Tally asked him again on his next pay day. Lonny,

who was then making about fifty dollars a week working for a ca-
terer, wordlessly gave the money to Tally and turned to the pinball
machine.

A few days later, on a Saturday night, Tally and Lonny, along
with several others, were going to a party. On the way they
stopped off at Lonny's mother's house so he could change his
clothes. In Lonny's presence, Lonny's mother told Tally of the difficulty she was having with Lonny, of how, despite his probation-
ary status, he had not been coming home at night, had not been
contributing toward his room and board, and had refused to repay
a loan to his brother. Lonny walked out of the room while she was
talking. Outside, Tally asked Lonny what this was all about. Lonny
told him simply that it was none of his business. Tally said that he
didn't know what the trouble was with Lonny, all he knew for
sure was that, "It ain't the same old Lonny."

The following week, complaining that he couldn't "make it"
with his family, especially his brother,[16] Lonny moved into a room
near the Carry-out shop. He went his way, and Tally went his.
When their paths crossed, as at a party or in the Carry-out shop,
their attempt to be casual with one another had an awkwardness
about it. It was clear that they had come a long way from that day
of backslapping camaraderie three and a half months earlier.

Tally and Bess, Earl, and Lucille—Bess was a tall, heavyset handsome
woman of twenty-three. She and her four children lived with her
mother in another section of the city. Tally was the father of Bess's
youngest child. Bess sometimes came to the corner on Tally's pay
day and waited for him to come home from work. She would tell
Tally she needed five or ten dollars for shoes or other expenses for
their child, Tally would give her the money, they'd go into the

---

16. "Mother," "brother," "sister," etc., were Lonny's own terms for the members
of his adoptive family. This is not an instance of pseudo-kinship. Lonny did not learn
that they were not his real family until he was eighteen. He and his "brothers" were
not "going for brothers"; they were brothers by [informal] adoption.

Carry-out shop and have a sandwich or a soda and then Tally would put her in a cab for home. Bess's visits steadily became more frequent. In June, Tally and Bess had again become lovers and Bess sometimes came on a Friday evening with their year-old son and the three of them would spend the weekend in Tally's room.

Toward the end of June, Tally also began going out with Lucille, a thirty-year-old woman who had formerly lived near the Carry-out but now lived in another section of the city with her twelve-year-old son. Before going out with Tally, Lucille had been considered Earl's girl friend.

The day after Tally and Lucille first went out together, Tally and Earl stopped speaking to each other. The next weekend, the jilted lovers, Earl and Bess, also paired off. In July, less than two weeks after Tally and Lucille had become lovers, Tally moved out of the Carry-out shop area and moved in with Lucille and her young son, saying simply that he had had an argument with Miss Carrie, his landlady.

For the next few weeks, despite his having moved out of the area, Tally continued to come to the Carry-out straight from work and spent most of the weekends in the neighborhood as well. He was enthusiastic about his relationship with Lucille but, protesting that he didn't care what Bess did or who she did it with, he insisted that Bess was really in love with him and had hinted to him that she wanted them to get back together again.

On a Friday night, Earl and Bess were among a group of people standing on the corner outside the Carry-out shop. Tally walked onto the corner and asked Bess if he could speak to her privately. Bess followed Tally to the edge of a vacant lot about ten or twelve steps away. Tally turned to face her, then slapped her, knocked her to the ground, and began kicking her. Earl jumped to Bess's defense. Tally had been drinking and Earl, who searched for his knife but couldn't find it, fought Tally to a standoff. Both men ended up with torn clothing and scratches and bruises about the face, neck and arms, but neither was seriously hurt. Over the next several days, when Tally and Earl happened to be in the Carry-out shop or on the street at the same time, Tally ostentatiously ignored Earl. Earl looked at Tally with a hostile, watchful stare, and was careful not to turn his back on him.

One week later, Bess agreed to another meeting with Tally. Carrying Tally's son in her arms and holding her three-year-old daughter by the hand, Bess went to Nancy's place where she had agreed to meet Tally. Tally joined her there, and as they talked and drank, he bounced his son on his knee. Someone asked him his son's name. Tally stammered, then blurted "Sweetpea." Bess, in half-seriousness, slapped him across his face, saying wasn't that a shame for a man not to know his own son's name.

When Tally walked out of the room for a minute, Bess talked about her feelings for him. She liked him, she said. They had always had a lot of fun together, but she was sick and tired of his jealousy and getting slapped around every time he got drunk. If it happens again, she said, she was through. She said she had told Tally this before agreeing to come here tonight and he promised it wouldn't happen again.

When Tally returned, he and Bess danced and had a couple of drinks. Bess shook with laughter as Tally clowned the part of the contrite and ardent lover. At about ten o'clock Bess and the children went home. Tally was exuberant.

"She's going to put Earl down," he announced, and explained that Bess had told him that Earl was just a boy and that she wanted Tally because he was her man, and because "You know where it's at." Tally said that he had always loved Bess and wanted to marry her.

The next night, Tally, Earl and Richard were among the men and women in Nancy's place drinking and dancing. Earl and Richard walked out, followed a few minutes later by Tally.

Ten minutes after Tally had gone out, a woman ran into Nancy's place and announced that Tally had just been arrested. Outside, police cars and other emergency vehicles were pulling away, their red lights still flashing. Several groups of people were milling around on the street. Bess, Richard and Earl were standing together.

Richard said Tally was in real trouble this time. Bess said that a few minutes earlier she had accidentally met Tally on the streetcorner. She said he asked her to go with him and she refused. They argued, Tally slapped her, and Bess, repeating that she had determined not to be slapped again, pulled a beer can-opener out of her purse and raked his face with it. A policeman and a dog appeared. The policeman grabbed at Tally as Bess ran up the street. She said she drifted back when the police car arrived. Tonk joined the group and said that Tally had hit the policeman. Bess shrugged her shoulders, then she and Earl walked down the street together.[17]

Tally posted collateral and was released the next morning. He continued coming to the neighborhood on an occasional Friday or Saturday night, but he stayed away from the Carry-out shop. By the end of August one could spend several days on the corner or in the Carry-out shop and hear no mention of his name.

Although all these relationships are selections from Tally's network, it is important to note that it was not only Tally's network that was constantly being restructured. Tally is just as much a part of Richard's network as Richard is of his. A change in Tally's relationship with Richard, therefore, is not only a change in Tally's network of personal relationships but is also a change of the same order and magnitude in Richard's network of personal relationships. This kind of change is reciprocal and symmetrical: when Tally loses Richard as a friend, Richard loses Tally as a friend.

Other changes—asymmetrical and relatively unpredictable—also reverberate through associated networks. Tally's love affair with Emma Lou brings him and Richard closer together but his affair with Lucille draws him and Earl apart. And when Earl, in

---

17. This was the last time I ever saw Bess.

turn, began going out with Bess, the two men, who had been good friends, moved out to the edges of one another's networks.

It often happens, too, that changes in how people feel and act toward one another have important structural consequences for neighbor and kin groups, household, family and other social structures that are built up out of these personal relationships. When Richard and Tally get "up tight," Tally becomes a sometime member of Richard's household, sleeping there at night and acting as if it's "his home, his kitchen, his food." Emma Lou joins the household by way of her kinship tie with Shirley and Richard. Her affair with Tally brings Tally even closer into the household. The fight changes the composition of the household, literally overnight, and Shirley and Richard's kinship tie with Emma Lou is effectively broken.[18] Emma Lou moves in with Tally but soon his changed relationship with her forces her into a tenant–landlord relationship with Miss Carrie, and on this the two women build a friend relationship. Finally, her rejection by Tally drives her completely out of the neighborhood. Tally, meanwhile, either because of an argument with Miss Carrie or because of his attraction to Lucille, or both, moves in with Lucille. Lucille and her son, who had had only each other, now share their home with a man who acts as husband and father.

In general, Tom's relationship with Dick is independent of either of their relationships with Harry. As a rule, then, a change in a given relationship between two persons means only a simple

---

18. A dramatic and clear-cut instance of the way in which personal relationships can structure kinship ties was reported tearfully by Shirley. Richard had been in jail a week. Shirley was desperate for her children and herself and telephoned her sister in Philadelphia, hoping to borrow some money. Her sister, who had had a serious falling out with Richard, asked, "Is this the Shirley who calls herself Shirley Hawkins? Married to Richard Hawkins?" Shirley said yes. "Then you're not my sister," her sister told her. "My sister don't live with Richard Hawkins anymore [meaning, I won't recognize you as my sister unless and until you leave Richard]." And she hung up.

change in their respective networks and has no effect on networks other than their own. There are exceptions, however; sometimes a change in one network can have repercussions for networks that are two or more degrees removed. Indeed, if traced out in sufficient detail, an especially violent change, such as Tally's fight with Richard, may appear to send a shudder through a large part of the streetcorner system and force a whole series of adjustive realignments.

The overall picture is one of a broad web of interlocking, overlapping networks in which the incumbents are constantly—however irregularly—shifting and changing positions relative to one another. This fluidity and change which characterizes personal relationships is reflected in neighbor and kin relationships, in family, household, indeed in the whole social structure of the streetcorner world which rests to so large an extent precisely on the primary, face-to-face relationships of the personal network.[19]

In support of the economic, social and psychological forces arrayed against the stability of personal networks is the intrinsic weakness of friendship itself. Whether as cause, effect, or both, the fact is that friendships are not often rooted in long term associations nor do the persons involved necessarily know anything of

---

19. "Were [William F.] Whyte to return today to the cornervilles of America, he would probably find much less evidence of what he called 'highly organized and integrated' patterns of slum life." Richard A. Cloward and Lloyd E. Ohlin, *Delinquency and Opportunity: A Theory of Delinquent Gangs*, p. 210. On p. 172 of the same work, vertical and geographic mobility, housing and changing land use are identified as some of "the many forces making for instability in the social organization of some slum areas. . . . Forces of this kind keep a community off balance, for tentative efforts to develop social organization are quickly checked. *Transiency and instability become the overriding features of social life.*" (Emphasis added.) Whyte himself points out the importance of distinguishing between relatively stable slum communities (such as his own Street Corner Society) and unstable slum districts. He notes that Margaret Chandler, in "The Social Organization of Workers in a Rooming House Area," found that "an acquaintance of a week might be described as an old friend, so rapidly did the ties shift" ("On Street Corner Society," p. 257),

one another's personal history prior to their association.[20] The man would like to think—and sometimes says—that his friendship with so-and-so goes back several years or even into childhood—but this is not often the case in fact.[21] Their relationship rests almost entirely in present time. A man may have detailed knowledge of his friend's present circumstances and relationships but little else. He knows from the fact that his friend is on the street, and he knows, from looking into himself, the gross characteristic features of the friend's personal history. He knows his friend was raised principally by women and that he holds these women dearly, that he was brought up to love and fear God, that he's had little formal education, that he has few if any job skills and has worked in different towns and cities, that in one or more of these towns he fathered a child whom he has probably never seen, that he first came here because he has an uncle or aunt here, or because he met this girl, or because he heard about this job, or because he was wanted by the police or someone else wherever he used to live. But he does not know the particulars. He does not know whether it was his mother, grandmother or father's sister who raised him, how far he went in school, which towns and which cities he's lived and worked in, and what crucial experiences he had there, and so forth. Of course, much of this comes out as unsolicited, incidental information in the course of casual talk and hanging around, but much does not.[22] Especially lacking is an exchange of secret thoughts, of private hopes and fears.

---

20. Oscar Lewis found that "in some villages, peasants can live out their lives without any deep knowledge or understanding of the people whom they 'know' in face to face relationships" ("Further Observations on the Folk-Urban Continuum and Urbanization with Special Reference to Mexico City," p. 12)

21. When Leroy, for example, appeared as a character witness at Richard's murder trial, he testified that he had known Richard since they were kids. Leroy later protested that this was a minor exaggeration and shook his head in disbelief and wonderment when he was reminded that he did not meet Richard until the winter of 1961.

22. Not even their last names. One evening Richard was sitting in his apartment lamenting his present circumstances. He was reminded that he had a lot of friends

Friendship thus appears as a relationship between two people who, in an important sense, stand unrevealed to one another. Lacking depth in both past and present, friendship is easily uprooted by the tug of economic or psychological self-interest or by external forces acting against it.

The recognition of this weakness, coupled with the importance of friendship as a source of security and self-esteem, is surely a principal source of the impulse to romanticize relationships, to upgrade them, to elevate what others see as a casual acquaintanceship to friendship, and friendship to close friendship. It is this, perhaps, that lies behind the attempt to ascribe a past to a relationship that never had one, and to borrow from the bony structure of kinship ("going for brothers") to lend structural support to a relationship sorely in need of it. It is as if friendship is an artifact of desire, a wish relationship, a private agreement between two people to act "as if," rather than a real relationship between persons.

(he had been the janitor in his apartment house for five or six months). Richard snorted and said that if the police were to pick him up and allow him his one phone call, he wouldn't know what to do with it because he doesn't even know anyone's last name. This was not entirely true, but it clearly points up his own contemptuous assessment of the depths of the friendships he had formed in the Carry-out neighborhood. The quality of these friendships contrasted sharply with those he had formed in his hometown (1960 population: 1,100), where his family knew all the other Negro families and was known by them, and where his friends were young men and women he had known from infancy. See also p. 122.

CONCLUSION

This study has been primarily concerned with the inside world of the streetcorner Negro man, the world of daily, face-to-face relationships with wives, children, friends, lovers, kinsmen and neighbors. An attempt was made to see the man as he sees himself, to compare what he says with what he does, and to explain his behavior as a direct response to the conditions of lower-class Negro life rather than as mute compliance with historical or cultural imperatives.[1]

---

1. There is, fortunately, a growing suspicion that "culture" and "historical continuity" may not be the most useful constructs for dealing with lower-class behavior. Hylan Lewis, for example, suggests that "It is probably more fruitful to think of lower class families reacting in various ways to the facts of their position and to relative isolation rather than to the imperatives of a lower class culture" ("Culture, Class, and the Behavior of Low Income Families," p. 43). Richard Cloward and Lloyd Ohlin argue that "The historical-continuity theory of lower-class values . . . ignores the extent to which lower-class and delinquent cultures today are *predictable responses to conditions in our society rather than persisting patterns . . ."* (*Delinquency and Opportunity: A Theory of Delinquent Gangs,* p. 75; emphasis added.) Thomas Gladwin has similar misgivings: "Defining the multiproblem population as a subculture is only one of several ways of looking at the problem . . . the formulation is useful only if it can bring us closer to a solution" ("The Anthropologist's View of Poverty," p. 75). Elizabeth Bott challenges outright the use of the culture concept as an explanatory device: "I do not believe it is sufficient to explain variations . . . as cultural or sub-

This inside world does not appear as a self-contained, self-generating, self-sustaining system or even subsystem with clear boundaries marking it off from the larger world around it. It is in continuous, intimate contact with the larger society—indeed, is an integral part of it—and is no more impervious to the values, sentiments and beliefs of the larger society than it is to the blue welfare checks or to the agents of the larger society, such as the policeman, the police informer, the case worker, the landlord, the dope pusher, the Tupperware demonstrator, the numbers backer or the anthropologist.

One of the major points of articulation between the inside world and the larger society surrounding it is in the area of employment. The way in which the man makes a living and the kind of living he makes have important consequences for how the man sees himself and is seen by others; and these, in turn, importantly shape his relationships with family members, lovers, friends and neighbors.

Making a living takes on an overriding importance at marriage. The young, lower-class Negro gets married in his early twenties, at approximately the same time and in part for the same reason as his white or Negro working- or middle-class counterpart. He has no special motive for getting married; sex is there for the taking, with or without marriage, and he can also live with a woman or have children—if he has not done this already—without getting married. He wants to be publicly, legally married, to support a family and be the head of it, because this is what it is to be a man in our society, whether one lives in a room near the Carry-out or in an elegant house in the suburbs.

Although he wants to get married, he hedges on his commitment from the very beginning because he is afraid, not of marriage

---

cultural differences. To say that people behave differently or have different expectations because they belong to different cultures amounts to no more than saying that they behave differently—or that cultures are different because they are different" (*Family and Social Network*, p. 218).

itself, but of his own ability to carry out his responsibilities as husband and father. His own father failed and had to "cut out," and the men he knows who have been or are married have also failed or are in the process of doing so. He has no evidence that he will fare better than they and much evidence that he will not. However far he has gone in school he is illiterate or almost so; however many jobs he has had or hard he has worked, he is essentially unskilled.[2] Armed with models who have failed, convinced of his own worthlessness, illiterate and unskilled, he enters marriage and the job market with the smell of failure all around him. Jobs are only intermittently available. They are almost always menial, sometimes hard, and never pay enough to support a family.

In general, the menial job lies outside the job hierarchy and promises to offer no more tomorrow than it does today. The Negro menial worker remains a menial worker so that, after one or two or three years of marriage and as many children, the man who could not support his family from the very beginning is even less able to support it as time goes on. The longer he works, the longer he is unable to live on what he makes. He has little vested interest in such a job and learns to treat it with the same contempt held for it by the employer and society at large. From his point of view, the job is expendable; from the employer's point of view, he is. For reasons real or imagined, perhaps so slight as to go unnoticed by others, he frequently quits or is fired. Other times, he is jobless simply because he cannot find a job.

He carries this failure home where his family life is undergoing a parallel deterioration. His wife's adult male models also failed as husbands and fathers and she expects no less from him. She hopes but does not expect him to be a good provider, to make of them a family and be head of it, to be "the man of the house." But his failure to do these things does not make him easier to live with

---

2. And he is black. Together, these make a deadly combination and relegate him to the very bottom of our society.

because it was expected. She keys her demands to her wants, to her hopes, not to her expectations. Her demands mirror the man both as society says he should be and as he really is, enlarging his failure in both their eyes.

Sometimes he sits down and cries at the humiliation of it all. Sometimes he strikes out at her or the children with his fists, perhaps to lay hollow claim to being man of the house in the one way left open to him, or perhaps simply to inflict pain on this woman who bears witness to his failure as a husband and father and therefore as a man. Increasingly he turns to the streetcorner where a shadow system of values constructed out of public fictions serves to accommodate just such men as he, permitting them to be men once again provided they do not look too closely at one another's credentials.[3]

At the moment his streetcorner relationships take precedence over his wife and children he comes into his full inheritance bequeathed him by his parents, teachers, employers and society at large. This is the step into failure from which few if any return,

---

3. This "shadow system" of values is very close to Hyman Rodman's "value stretch." Members of the lower class, he says, "share the general values of the society with members of other classes, but in addition they have stretched these values, or developed alternative values, which help them adjust to their deprived circumstances" ("The Lower-Class Value Stretch," p. 209).

I would add at least two qualifications to Rodman's and other formulations that posit an alternate system of lower-class values. The first is that the stretched or alternative value systems are not the same order of values, either phenomenologically or operationally, as the parent or general system of values: they are derivative, subsidiary in nature, thinner and less weighty, less completely internalized, and seem to be value images reflected by forced or adaptive behavior rather than real values with a positive determining influence on behavior of choice. The second qualification is that the alternative value system is not a distinct value system which can be separately invoked by its users. It appears only in association with the parent system and is separable from it only analytically. Derivative, insubstantial, and co-occurring with the parent system, it is as if the alternative value system is a shadow cast by the common value system in the distorting lower-class setting. Together, the two systems lie behind much that seems paradoxical and inconsistent, familiar and alien, to the middle-class observer from his one-system perspective.

and it is at this point that the rest of society can wring its hands or rejoice in the certain knowledge that he has ended up precisely as they had predicted he would.

The streetcorner is, among other things, a sanctuary for those who can no longer endure the experience or prospect of failure. There, on the streetcorner, public fictions support a system of values which, together with the value system of society at large, make for a world of ambivalence, contradiction and paradox, where failures are rationalized into phantom successes and weaknesses magically transformed into strengths. On the streetcorner, the man chooses to forget he got married because he wanted to get married and assume the duties, responsibilities and status of manhood; instead, he sees himself as the "put-upon" male who got married because his girl was pregnant or because he was tricked, cajoled or otherwise persuaded into doing so. He explains the failure of his marriage by the "theory of manly flaws." Conceding that to be head of a family and to support it is a principal measure of a man, he claims he was too much of a man to be a man. He says his marriage did not fail because he failed as breadwinner and head of the family but because his wife refused to put up with his manly appetite for whiskey and other women, appetites which rank high in the scale of shadow values on the streetcorner.[4]

Outside of marriage, he sees himself as a ruthless Exploiter of Women. Where women are concerned, he says, a man should take what he can get when he can get it. He claims not to understand men who do otherwise. Establishing his claim in word or deed to being an Exploiter of Women frees him to enter into a love relationship with one or more women, to declare publicly his love for them and to attempt to deal with them on the nonexploitative basis of mutual respect.

---

4. "The behaviors of lower class persons which are considered deviant, either by the members of their own groups or by the larger society, can be regarded as efforts to attain some sense of valid identity, as efforts to gratify the prompting of needs from inside and to elicit a response of recognition as valid persons from those around them." Lee Rainwater, "Work and Identity in the Lower Class (forthcoming)."

In practice, however, he cannot keep separate the exploitative and nonexploitative relationships. As exploiter, his actions sometimes fit his words but just as often he turns away women who offer him their bodies or their money, or he treats them with a solicitousness for their welfare which unmasks the uncompromising Exploiter of Women as a pretentious fraud. Similarly, his sincere profession of undying love for a woman and his offer to put himself and his goods at her everlasting disposal do not long hold up under the weight of his need for money, his desire to consume his own goods, or his desire to confirm his manliness by other conquests. Thus, despite the man's inability or unwillingness to conduct himself as a wholly exploitative animal, the exploitative impulse—supported by the man's poverty of material and inner resources and by the public fiction of man as Exploiter of Women—remains sufficiently strong to compromise the quality and foreshorten the life of man-woman relationships. The result is that man-woman relationships tend to be relatively brief, one-sided affairs which come to an abrupt and frequently violent end.

Conflicts of interest and a general dearth of material and inner resources eat away at the whole structure of personal relationships. Friendships are precious relationships and of special importance to one's sense of physical and emotional security. Ideally, friendship is seen as a system of mutual aid in which the movement of money, goods, services and emotional support flows freely out of loyalty and generosity and according to need rather than as a mutual exchange resting securely on a quid pro quo basis. But money, goods and the stuff of comfort are normally in short supply, obliging each man to keep careful if secret account of what he gives out and takes in. Moreover, each man knows that his own and his friends' resources are meager and that, unconditional pledges of mutual aid notwithstanding, each will ultimately have to look to himself whenever he requires more than token assistance or aid of the kind that would materially deplete the resources of the giver. And he knows, too, that all friendships are vulnerable to the sudden clash of self-interest, especially where sex and money are concerned.

As if in anticipation of the frailty of personal relationships—to get as much as he can from them while they last and perhaps hopefully to prolong them—the man hurries each relationship toward a maximum intensity, quickly up-grading casual acquaintances to friends, and friends to best friends and lovers. This rush to upgrade personal relationships, to hurry them on to increasingly intense levels of association, may itself contribute to a foreshortening of their life span, prematurely loading the incumbents with expectations and obligations which their hastily constructed relationships simply cannot support.[5]

The fluidity of personal relationships appears, at another level, as a fluidity in neighbor and kin groups and in families and households which are built up out of these personal relationships. Indeed, transience is perhaps the most striking and pervasive characteristic of this streetcorner world. It characterizes not only the subtler social relationships but the more obvious spatial relationships as well. It characterizes not only the relationships of those within the network of interlocking and overlapping personal communities at any given time but also the movement into and out of these networks. Some men come into this particular area to escape police who have chased them out from another. Some men leave for the same reason. Some men, like Tally, leave the area because they have used up their friendships and alliances and have to start anew elsewhere. But at the same time, another Tally has moved out of his old area and into this one for the same reasons. Here a family is evicted and the sidewalk becomes a staging area for the allocation of the individual family members to households in the same area or in a distant state. The next day or the same day, the same room or apartment is taken over by members of a family

---

5. From this point of view, the primary function of pseudo-kinship is to anticipate the frailty of personal relationships by attempting to invest them with the durables of kinship.

evicted from another part of the city. Here a man loses a job and moves out; another finds one and moves in. Here is a man released from prison after seven years and there goes a man who wants to try his luck in New York. Traffic is heavy in all directions.

Thus, this streetcorner world does not at all fit the traditional characterization of the lower-class neighborhood as a tightly knit community whose members share the feeling that "we are all in this together." Nor does it seem profitable—especially for those who would see it changed—to look at it as a self-supporting, on-going social system with its own distinctive "design for living," principles of organization, and system of values.

Whether the world of the lower-class Negro should be seen as a distinctive subculture or as an integral part of the larger society (at the bottom of it, perhaps, but as much a part of it as those in the middle or on top) is much more than an academic question and has important consequences for "intervention." Marriage among lower-class Negroes, for example, has been described as "serial monogamy," a pattern in which the woman of childbearing age has a succession of mates during her procreative years. The label "serial monogamy" clearly has a cultural referent, deriving as it does from the traditional nomenclature used to designate cultur-ally distinctive patterns of marriage, such as polygyny, polyandry, monogamy, and so on. "Serial monogamy," then, as against the unqualified monogamous ideal of American society at large, refers to and *is used as evidence for* the cultural separateness and distinctive-ness of the urban, lower-class Negro.

When these same phenomena are examined directly in the larger context of American life, both "serial monogamy" and cul-tural distinctiveness tend to disappear. In their place is the same pattern of monogamous marriage found elsewhere in our society but one that is characterized by failure. The woman does not have a simple "succession of mates during her procreative years." She has a husband and he a wife, and their hopes and their intentions—if not their expectations—are that this will be a durable, permanent union. More often, however, it is their fears rather than their hopes which materialize. The marriage fails and they part, he to become one of a "succession of mates" taken by woman whose husband has left her, and she to accept one or more men. While these secondary and subsequent liaisons are, for the most part, somewhat pale reflections of the formal marriage relationship, each is modeled after it and fails for much the same reasons as does marriage itself. From this perspective, then, the succession of mates which characterizes marriage among lower-class Negroes does not constitute a distinctive cultural pattern "with an integrity of its own." It is rather the cultural model of the larger society as seen through the prism of repeated failure. Indeed, it might be more profitable—again, especially for those concerned with changing it—to look on marriage here as a succession of failures rather than as a succession of mates.[6]

In summary, what is challenged here is not that the marriage pattern among urban low-income Negroes does not involve a "succession of mates" but the implication that this succession of mates constitutes prima facie evidence for the cultural distinctiveness of those to whom it is attributed.

Much of what has been dealt with in the foregoing chapters can be looked at from this same point of view. From this perspective, the streetcorner man does not appear as a carrier of an independent cultural tradition. His behavior appears not so much as a way of realizing the distinctive goals and values of his own subculture, or of conforming to its models, but rather as his way of trying to achieve many of the goals and values of the larger society, of

---

6. "It is important that we not confuse basic life chances and actual behavior with basic cultural values and preferences. . . . The focus of efforts to change should be on background conditions and on precipitants of the deviant behaviors rather than on presumably different class or cultural values." Hylan Lewis, "Culture, Class and the Behavior of Low Income Families," p. 43.

failing to do this, and of concealing his failure from others and from himself as best he can.[7]

If, in the course of concealing his failure, or of concealing his fear of even trying, he pretends—through the device of public fictions—that he did not want these things in the first place and claims that he has all along been responding to a different set of rules and prizes, we do not do him or ourselves any good by accepting this claim at face value.

Such a frame of reference, I believe, can bring into clearer focus the practical points of leverage for social change in this area. We do not have to see the problem in terms of breaking into a puncture proof circle, of trying to change values, of disrupting the lines of communication between parent and child so that parents cannot make children in their own image, thereby transmitting their culture inexorably, ad infinitum. No doubt, each generation does provide role models for each succeeding one. Of much greater importance for the possibilities of change, however, is the fact that many similarities between the lower-class Negro father and son (or mother and daughter) do not result from "cultural transmission" but from the fact that the son goes out and independently experiences the same failures, in the same areas, and for much the same reasons as his father. What appears as a dynamic, self-sustaining cultural process is, in part at least, a relatively simple piece of social machinery which turns out, in rather mechanical fashion, independently produced look-alikes. The problem is how to change the conditions which, by guaranteeing failure, cause the son to be made in the image of the father.

Taking this viewpoint does not reduce the magnitude of the problem but does serve to place it in the more tractable context of economics, politics and social welfare. It suggests that poverty is, indeed, a proper target in the attempt to bring lower-class Negroes

---

7. ". . . concealment and ego-protection are of the essence of social intercourse." Everett C. Hughes, *Men and Their Work*, p. 43.

"into the mainstream of American life," and it supports the long line of social scientists, from E. Franklin Frazier and Gunnar Myrdal down through Kenneth Clark and Richard Cloward, in seeing the inability of the Negro man to earn a living and support his family as the central fact of lower-class Negro life. If there is to be a change in this way of life, this central fact must be changed; the Negro man, along with everyone else, must be given the skills to earn a living and an opportunity to put these skills to work.

No one pretends that this is an easy matter, to be accomplished at one fell stroke. For many Negro men, jobs alone are no longer enough. Before he can earn a living, he must believe that he can do so, and his women and children must learn to believe this along with him. But he finds it difficult to begin without their support, and they find it difficult to give their support until he begins. The beginning, then, will doubtless be a slow one, but, once started, success will feed on itself just as failure has done.[8] A beginning must be made, however, and it must be made simultaneously at all points in the life cycle. Children and young people must have good schools and good teachers who can give them the skills and the training to compete for jobs and careers, and they must have teachers who believe in them and help them believe in themselves. Jobs that pay enough to support a family must be opened up to the adult generation so that they can support their families, so that the young people can see the changed reality, so that young and old can experience it and gain a vested interest in the world they live in.[9]

---

8. "Feed upon one another" suggests the model of "the vicious circle"—the model which served as Gunnar Myrdal's main explanatory scheme for analyzing the Negro problem in the U.S. In *An American Dilemma*, pp. 1065ff, the model of the vicious circle—refined as the Principal of Accumulation—is treated in detail. "The theory of the vicious circle is a cause rather for optimism than pessimism. The cumulative principle works both ways." (P. 1069n, emphasis added.)

9. For some adults, perhaps many, it will be too late, but we will not know for which ones until it is tried for all. Those for whom it is too late should be bought off, with cash or sinecures, in much the same way and for much the same reasons as

Despite the many differences of opinion about how these things are to be achieved, the real problem lies elsewhere. Hundreds of research and demonstration projects have established that we have the know-how to effect these changes. Under the aegis of the Office of Economic Opportunity, a multitude of programs designed to achieve these ends are already under way and some have begun to have a discernible beneficial effect on selected groups and individuals.

What is lacking is not know-how and programs but a clarity of purpose, of motive, and of intention. What do we want to do, why do we want to do it, and how much are we willing to pay for it (not so much in money but in terms of basic changes in the class and racist structure of our society) remain largely unanswered questions.

There are those, for example, who say that what we want to do is eliminate poverty from our national life, but these same people throw their hands up in horror when it is suggested that a guaranteed annual wage would go a long way toward doing just that. Others are more concerned with life styles than with poverty per se. They would use the poverty program to give money, advice, and "enrichment" programs to those among the poor who are willing to adopt (what are presumed to be peculiarly) middle-class styles of behavior, and thereby reduce crime, child neglect, etc. Still others would use the poverty program as a carrot-and-stick device to sort out the deserving and nondeserving poor, giving handouts to one group, making war on the other. There is also abroad in the land a concern that we may go too far and upset the relationship between different segments of our society which

the Germans pay reparations to survivors of the Nazi persecutions or as we pay reparations to Japanese Americans disenfranchised, unpropertied, and interned during the war, or as our society sometimes indemnifies men wrongly imprisoned. It is a very small price to pay for their cooperation or neutrality, and there is comfort to be gained from the fact that, in this way, we may not have to buy off generation after generation as we do under our present welfare programs.

presumably now work together for the good of the whole. This concern is most frequently expressed by those with an immediate vested interest in the availability of a pool of low-skilled labor. Their argument draws much of its strength from sophisticated analyses and observations such as this one by Walter Miller:

> The fundamental questions are: How large a low-skilled laboring force does our society require? . . . From what sources are we to get the incumbents of these jobs, and where are they to receive the socialization and training needed to execute them? Under existing circumstances, the female-based child-rearing unit is a prime source of this essential pool of low-skilled laborers. It brings them into the world, and it furnishes them the values, the aspirations, and the psychic make up that low-skill jobs require (e g , high toleration of recurrent unemployment; high boredom tolerance; high flexibility with respect to work, residence, relational patterns; capacity to find life gratification outside the world of work).[10]

These are, indeed, fundamental questions, and the maintenance of the lower classes as they are presently ordered is one way of answering them. This solution, however, in which those who are to be at the bottom of our society are selected while they are still in the womb violates every hope and promise this nation has held out to its people.

Moreover, if "high boredom tolerance . . . flexibility" and "capacity to find life gratification outside the world of work" are understood to mean that people at the bottom of our society are content with their lot, even happy with it, this understanding represents a grave misreading of history and recent events and leads to the assumption that the impetus to change their life circumstances comes not from the lower classes themselves but from moralists, humanitarians, politicians, and others on the outside. Persons in-

---

10. Foreword to Sydney E. Bernard, *Fatherless Families: Their Economic and Social Adjustment.*

volved in poverty programs may even congratulate themselves on their humanitarian work, claiming to be helping people who have not even asked for it. The following passage, for example, appeared in the foreword to a widely circulated manual for training subprofessional aides among the poor. Speaking of the national anti-poverty and community mental health programs, the authors say:

> It is to the credit of professional and political leaders that both these programs have come into existence as a result of their sense of social responsibility, their vision and initiative, without the stimulus of a vocal and organized demand from the suffering people themselves.[11]

Self-deception such as this simply will not do. It is precisely the discontent of the poor, and their expression of it, which lie behind recent attempts to change the life conditions of the poor. The refusal to see clearly and state frankly the self-serving character of recent efforts to assist those at the bottom of our society is a disservice to everyone concerned and stands in the way of real progress. If Negroes had to wait upon the good will and largesse of professional and political leaders—which they will not and are not doing—they would have to wait, to put it conservatively, a long time. There is undoubtedly much goodwill among white middle-class persons; there always has been, but it was never (and is not now) sufficiently widespread and deep-rooted as to constitute an invitation—much less a helping hand—to Negroes to come and share in the good things in our society. Of much more importance than goodwill is the increasing awareness of self-interest, the growing certainty that unless Negroes are permitted, even encouraged, to share in these things, neither we nor our children shall continue to enjoy them.

---

11. Robert Reiff and Frank Riessman, "The Indigenous Nonprofessional: A Strategy of Change in Community Action and Community Mental Health Programs," p. 1.

In a sense, we have already forfeited the power to initiate action in this area. The moral initiative has long passed over to Negroes and political initiative seems to be moving in that direction, too. This may be a disquieting, even fearful development to some segments of our society. In the long run, however, the sooner and the more effectively Negroes organize to promote their own self-interests, just as other ethnic and religious groups and the working class have done before them, the sooner and more effectively we can get on to other problems standing in the way of building a democratic society.

Since the great power lies with the white middle class, great decisions have to be made as to how this power is to be used in responding to action and demands initiated by the Negro masses and articulated by their leaders. Most of the time, the great federal power will best be used in direct support of the actionists. On some occasions, such as the outbreak at Watts, restraint will be the most judicious if difficult use of that great power.

In searching for guidelines to help us shape our responses, we would do well to keep in mind W. H. Auden's admonition to twentieth century man:

We must love one another or die.

Perhaps this is too much to ask of ourselves and others. Perhaps it will be enough if we just act as if we do.

APPENDIX:
A FIELD EXPERIENCE
IN RETROSPECT

Robert read the book slowly and with feeling, pausing only occasionally to take a swig of gin and chase it quickly with some beer. Lonny listened quietly and watched with blinking eyes as Robert changed his voice for each of the characters, assuming a falsetto for Snow White. But my own interest started to wander, probably because I had already read the book and seen the movie.

Suddenly Robert raised his voice and startled me back into attention. I looked at Lonny—placid, eye-blinking Lonny—and at Ronald—a handkerchief around his head and a gold earring stuck in his left ear making him look like a storybook pirate—and wondered what the hell I was doing there with these two guys, drinking gin and beer and listening to *Snow White and the Seven Dwarfs*.

I thought back to the events leading up to this situation. From this perspective, everything looked normal and reasonable. I retrieved my can of beer, sat back and listened to the rest of the story. Robert gave it a damn fine reading.

[Field Note, April 1962]

This chapter, in slightly different form, was originally written for the Child Rearing Study of the Health and Welfare Council of the National Capital Area.

BACKGROUND

When I came to the Child Rearing Study Project on January 1, 1962, this NIMH-supported study of "Child Rearing Practices Among Low Income Families in the District of Columbia" was well into its third year. My job was to collect field material on low-income adult males to complement the data already secured through family interviews.

From the very beginning I felt comfortable with the prospect of working with lower-class Negroes. I was born and raised in Washington, D.C. My father and mother were both Jewish immigrants from Eastern Europe—my mother from Latvia, my father from Russia. My father was a grocer and we lived in rooms above or behind the various stores which he operated. All were in predominantly Negro neighborhoods.

School and playground were white, but all of our customers and most of the neighbors were Negroes. Among them and their children I had many acquaintances, several playmates and a few friends. The color line, retraced daily at school and playground and home, was always there; but so were my day-by-day contacts with Negro men, women and children in the store, on the street, and occasionally in their houses; watching a crap game in Sam's place; witnessing the Devil being exorcised from a woman writhing on the floor of a storefront church from my seat in the back row; shooting crap for pennies in a dark hallway; sitting with Benton on the curb, poking aimlessly at debris, waiting for something interesting to happen. It was not until I was seventeen and enlisted in the Marine Corps that I began to move in an almost exclusively white world.

PREPARING FOR THE FIELD

I spent the first week in familiarizing myself with the project and with the work that had already been done. I had several informal discussions with Dr. Hylan Lewis, the director of the project, and gradually gained a feeling for the kind of material that was wanted. Importantly, he laid down no hard-and-fast ground rules on the assumption that the job could best be done if I were free to feel my way around for a few weeks and discover for myself the techniques that were most congenial to me. His one prescription was that the work be securely anchored in the purposes of the project, remembering, too, that "Everything is grist for our mill." As I think back on this now, I see a clear connection between his instructions and his fondness for the quotation, "The scientific method is doing one's darndest with his brains, no holds barred."

Having partially digested the project literature, I told the director that I was ready to get started. He suggested a neighborhood that might be "a good place to get your feet wet." His instructions were: "Go out there and make like an anthropologist."

"Out there" was not at all like the Indian village of Winisk on Hudson Bay in which I had done field work. I was not at all sure how one "makes like an anthropologist" in this kind of "out there." Somewhat wistfully, perhaps, I thought how much neater things would be if anthropologists, as they had done in the early thirties, limited themselves to the study of "wholes," a tribe, a village, or some other social unit with distinct boundaries and small enough to be encompassed in its entirety by direct observation.

When I thought about just what I was going to do, I kept in mind the job Richard Slobodin had done for the Child Rearing Study in the summer of 1960.[1] As part of the effort to get at community as well as family influences in child rearing, the director had assigned Slobodin to "make like an anthropologist" in a one-block enclave in northwest Washington. It seemed to me that I could use his work as a model and, in the course of a year, produce several such studies, each covering a strategic part of the world of the low-income male. I thought of doing a neighborhood study,

---

1. Richard Slobodin, " 'Upton Square': A Field Report and Commentary."

then moving on say, to a construction laborers' union, then a bootleg joint, and perhaps rounding these out with a series of genealogies and life histories. I was going to give myself about a month or so of poking around town, getting the feel of things, before committing myself to any firm plan of action.

IN THE FIELD

In taking up the director's suggestion that this would be "a good place to get your feet wet," I went in so deep that I was completely submerged and my plan to do three or four separate studies, each with its own neat, clean boundaries, dropped forever out of sight. My initial excursions into the street—to poke around, get the feel of things, and to lay out the lines of my field work—seldom carried me more than a block or two from the corner where I started. From the very first weeks or even days, I found myself in the middle of things; the principal lines of my field work were laid out, almost without my being aware of it. For the next year or so, and intermittently thereafter, my base of operations was the corner Carry-out across the street from my starting point.

The first time out, I had gone less than one short block when I noticed a commotion up the street. A man—Detective Wesley, I learned later—was dragging a kicking, screaming woman to a police call box. A small crowd had gathered on each of the four corners to watch. I approached two men and asked what the woman had done. Both were uncertain. The younger of the two said that he had heard two stories and proceeded to tell me both of them, concluding with the observation that he had known Detective Wesley for six or seven years and that he was "nobody to fool with."

I said that sometimes being a cop seems to do something to a man. This led to a discussion of policemen and each of us contributed personal experiences or anecdotes on the subject. After ten or fifteen minutes of this, the older man said goodbye and walked off. The younger man stayed on. Across the street from where we were standing was the Downtown Cafe. I suggested that we go in and have some coffee and he agreed. As we walked across the street he asked if I was a policeman. I told him no and explained that I was working on a study of family life in the city. There was no more discussion about who I was or why I was there. We sat at the bar for several hours talking over coffee.

I had not accomplished what I set out to do, but this was only the first day. And, anyway, when I wrote up this experience that evening, I felt that it presented a fairly good picture of this young man and that most of the material was to the point. Tomorrow, I decided, I would go back to my original plan—nothing had been lost.

But tomorrow never came. At nine the next morning, I headed down the same street. Four men were standing in a group in front of the Carry-out.

> Three were winos, in their forties—all marked with old scars on face and neck, dressed shabbily, but sober. The fourth was a man of thirty-two or thirty-three, who looked as if he had just stepped out of a slick magazine advertisement. . . . One of the winos had a month-old puppy stuck in the front of his overcoat. Only the dog's head was exposed
>
> The group approached me and one of the older men said, "Isn't he a nice puppy?" I said yes, and began patting the dog. "He just bought him," one man said. "I wanted the female, too, to breed them," said the man holding the dog, "but that woman, she sold the female to her friend."
>
> The puppy was whining. "Maybe it's hungry," said the older man, "let's get him some hamburger." "No man, he'll get worms from that stuff," said one of the others. I suggested milk and we all went into the Carry-out. I asked the waitress for a half pint of milk. The man asked for a saucer. "You can't feed him here," the waitress said, "the Health Department would close us up." She gave us a

paper plate and the milk (paid for by me). We took the dog into a hallway next door. Everyone was pleased at how eagerly the puppy drank.

A man who had been in the Carry-out joined us in the hallway. "That's a shepherd, isn't he? Just what I want for my little boy." I said, "I wish I could get one for my little girl, but she's allergic to all animals, dust, and lots of things." "It's better that way," said one of the winos. "She'll outgrow it. But man, if you don't have that until you're full grown—man, look out." "Yes, that's right," the newcomer agreed. "I know a woman who got allergies after she was grown and she got bronica asthma with it."

The dog finished the milk. The owner put him back in his overcoat and I shook hands all around with the winos. We split up three ways. The winos went up the street, the well-dressed man down the street, and the newcomer—who turned out to be Tally Jackson—and I went into the Carry-out.

For more than four hours Tally and I lounged around in the Carry-out, talking, drinking coffee, watching people come in and go out, watching other hangers-on as they bantered with the waitresses, horsed around among themselves, or danced to the jukebox. Everyone knew Tally and some frequently sought out his attention. Tally sometimes participated in the banter but we were generally left undisturbed when we were talking. When I left at two o'clock, Tally and I were addressing each other by first names ("Elliot" was strange to him and we settled for "Ellix") and I was able to address the two waitresses by their first names without feeling uncomfortable. I had also learned to identify several other men by their first names or nicknames, had gotten hints on personal relationships, and had a biographical sketch (part of it untrue I learned later) of Tally.

Back on the street, I ended up at the Downtown Cafe, this time by way of the morning's now very drunk owner of the puppy, who was standing near the entrance. The puppy was our bond and we talked about him with an enthusiasm that perhaps neither of us felt. Later, the well-dressed man who had also been part of the puppy episode came in and joined me at the bar. Then, still drinking beer at the bar stool, I met two other men in quick succession. The first man had to leave shortly for his night-shift busboy job at the restaurant. The other was a surly man in his middle thirties who initiated the contact by taking the stool next to me and asking what kind of work I did, adding that he had seen me around the day before, watching Detective Wesley drag that woman across the street.

I told him briefly what my job was.

"Well, if you hang around here you'll see it all. Anything can happen and it does happen here. It can get rough and you can get your head knocked in. You'll be okay though, if you know one or two of the right people."

"That's good to know," I told him, guessing (and hoping) that he was one of the "right people." He left me with the impression that he was being friendly and, in a left-handed sort of way, was offering me his protection.

By the end of the second day I had met nine men, learned the names of several more, and spent many hours in close public association with several men, at least two of whom were well known. And perhaps most important of all, in my own mind I had partly sloughed off that feeling of being a stranger and achieved that minimum sense of "belonging" which alone permits an ease of manner and mind so essential in building personal relationships.

Over the next three or four weeks, I made several excursions into other neighborhoods and followed up at the Downtown Cafe and the Carry-out shop on an irregular basis, getting to know some of the people better and many others for the first time. Frequently I ate breakfast and lunch at the Carry-out and began putting occasional dimes in the jukebox and in the pinball machine. Ted Moore, who worked at a liquor store nearby and whom I had first met in the Carry-out while he was waiting for the store to open, regularly alternated with me in buying coffee and doughnuts in the morning. At the Downtown Cafe the man who told me that I'd be okay if I knew "one or two of the right people" publicly identified me as his friend. ("Sure I know him," he told another man in my presence. "We had a long talk the other day. He's my friend and he's okay, man, he's okay. At first I thought he was a cop, but he's no cop. He's okay.")

All in all, I felt I was making steady progress. There was still plenty of suspicion and mistrust, however. At least two men who hung around the Carry-out—one of them the local numbers man—had seen me dozens of times in close quarters, but they kept their distance and I kept mine. Once, accidentally, I caught the numbers man's eye as I walked in. We held the stare for three or four seconds and I nodded slightly but he wouldn't let go. I went on about my business, determined that I wasn't going to be stared down next time and that he'd get no more nods from me unless he nodded first. As it turned out, I didn't have long to wait.

One mid-February day, I walked into the Carryout.

> . . . Tally was having a cup of coffee. "Look here," he said. "Where is this place?" Tally took out a sheet of paper from an envelope and handed it to me. It was a summons to appear as a witness for the defense in the case of the United States versus Lonny Reginald Small. A faint stamp indicated that Tally was to report to the United States District Court for the District of Columbia at 3rd and Pennsylvania Avenue, Northwest, at ten o'clock this morning. I read off the address. It was then 9:40. I suggested that Tally take a cab, but when Tally said he didn't have the money I offered to drive him down. He quickly accepted. On the way, Tally explained that Lonny was a friend of his. Lonny was being tried for murdering his wife last summer. "Lonny is a nice guy," he said. "He's one hundred percent."

Thus began a three-week odyssey into the world of Lonny Small, a young man of twenty-six who, according to the jury's subsequent verdict of "not guilty," had choked his wife to death accidentally. Upon his acquittal, Lonny was rearrested in the courthouse for a violation of probation (on a previous grand larceny conviction) in another jurisdiction. He waived extradition, was given a hearing, was released on an appearance bond, and after another hearing he was again placed on probation.

Almost imperceptibly, my association with Tally, and through him with Lonny, was projecting me into the role of a principal actor in Lonny's life. By being with Tally through the trial, I found that first Tally, then Lonny, were looking to me for leadership and, as in the question of waiving extradition, for decision making. Court officials, apparently taking their cues from Lonny, began looking to me as his spokesman.

The follow-up of Lonny, which took most of my time for at least the next two weeks, carried me into dozens of places and into contact with scores of people. Throughout this period I stayed in close touch with the project director, getting clearance for and weighing the possible consequences of my growing involvement with the authorities. I went to three different jails during this time, sat through one murder trial and two hearings in judges' chambers, testifying at one of them. I went to bondsmen's offices, to the United States Employment Service, to the Blessed Martin de Porres Hostel (for homeless men) and into several private homes. I met policemen, judges, lawyers, bondsmen, probation officers, and one of Lonny's former employers. I talked with his friends and at least one enemy, his mother-in-law, whose daughter he had killed. I met in council several times with various members of his extended family (who accepted me, through Tally, as Lonny's friend, no questions asked) in their houses, and drove around with them to the houses of other members of the family trying to raise money for Lonny's bond.

Meanwhile, back at the Carry-out, where Tally and I were meeting regularly at night and where I tried to stop in during the day whenever possible, people I had never seen, or others I had seen but never spoken to, began coming up to me and asking, "Is

Lonny out yet?" or "Did you raise his bail yet?" or simply, "How's it going?" Bumdoodle, the numbers man, one of those who had not known Lonny, was especially solicitous of Lonny's welfare. He, too, began calling me by my first name and, although I kept no record of it, I think it was at this time that he dropped all subterfuge in taking numbers in my presence and soon began taking bets from me.

By the middle of March, Tally and I were close friends ("up tight") and I was to let him know if I wanted or needed "anything, anytime." By April, the number of men whom I had come to know fairly well and their acceptance of me had reached the point at which I was free to go to the rooms or apartments where they lived or hung out, at almost any time, needing neither an excuse nor an explanation for doing so. Like other friends, I was there to pass the time, to hang around, to find out "what's happening."

I switched my day around to coincide with the day worker's leisure hours: from four in the afternoon until late at night, according to what was going on. Alone, or with one, two or half a dozen others, I went to poolrooms, to bars, or to somebody's room or apartment. Much of the time we just hung around the Carry-out, playing the pinball machine or standing on the corner watching the world go by. Regularly at five, I met my five "drinking buddies" when they came off from work and we went into a hallway for an hour or so of good drinking and easy talk.

Friday afternoon to Sunday night was especially exciting and productive. I'd go to Nancy's "place" (apartment) where, at almost any hour, one could get liquor, listen to music, or engage in conversation. Or perhaps seven or eight of us would buy some beer and whiskey and go up to Tonk's apartment near the Carry-out where he lived with his wife. Occasionally, I'd pair up with one or two men and go to a party, a movie, or a crap game, which might be in almost any part of town. Sunday afternoon was an especially good time to pick up news or happenings of the preceding forty-eight hours. People were generally rested up from the night before, relaxed, and ready to fill one another in on events which involved the police, breakups of husband-wife relations and bed-and-board arrangements, drink-stimulated brawls, sex adventures, and parties they had witnessed, heard about, or participated in over Friday and Saturday.

By April most people seemed to be taking it for granted that I belonged in the area. At least two men did not trust me or like me, but by then I was too strongly entrenched for them to challenge successfully my right to be there, even had they chosen to do so. New people moved into the area and I found myself being regarded as an old-timer, sometimes being asked to corroborate events which predated my arrival.

Throughout this period, my field observations were focused on individuals: what they said, what they did, and the contexts in which they said them or did them. I sought them out and was sought out by them.

My field notes contain a record of what I saw when I looked at Tally, Richard, Sea Cat and the others. I have only a small notion—and one that I myself consider suspect—of what they saw when they looked at me.

Some things, however, are very clear. They saw, first of all, a white man. In my opinion, this brute fact of color, as they understood it in their experience and as I understood it in mine, irrevocably and absolutely relegated me to the status of outsider. I am not certain, but I have a hunch that they were more continuously aware of the color difference than I was. When four of us sat around a kitchen table, for example, I saw three Negroes; each of them saw two Negroes and a white man.

Sometimes, when the word "nigger" was being used easily and conversationally or when, standing on the corner with several men, one would have a few words with a white passerby and call him a "white mother-fucker," I used to play with the idea that maybe I wasn't as much of an outsider as I thought. Other events, and later readings of the field materials, have disabused me of this particular touch of vanity.

Whenever the fact of my being white was openly introduced, it pointed up the distance between me and the other person, even when the intent of introducing it was, I believe, to narrow that distance.

> . . . All of us left Tally's room together. Tally grabbed my arm and pulled me aside near the storefront church and said, "I want to talk to you." With no further introduction, he looked me straight in the eye and started talking.
>
> "I'm a liar. I been lying to you all along now and I want to set it straight, even if it means we can't be friends no more. I only lied to you about one thing. Everything else I told you is gospel truth but I did lie about one thing and that makes me a liar. I know that some white people think that if you catch a man in a lie one time you can't never trust him after that. And even if you feel that way about it I still got to tell you. You remember when you first come around here, I told you. . . . Well, that was a lie. . . . I didn't think nothing of it at first, but then you and me started going around together and when we started getting real tight, my conscience started whomping me. I kept looking for a place to tell you but it never seemed right. Then tonight . . . I knew this was the right time. I knew you were going to find out and I didn't want you to find out from somebody else. . . ."

Once I was with Richard in his hometown. It was his first visit in five years. We arrived in the middle of the night and had to leave before daybreak because Richard was wanted by the local police. We were in his grandmother's house. Besides Richard, there were his grandmother, his aunt, and two unrelated men, both long-time friends of Richard.

The group was discussing the possibility of Richard's coming home to stay and weighing the probable consequences. In the middle of the discussion, Richard interrupted and nodded at me.

"Now Ellix here is white, as you can see, but he's one of my best friends. Him and me are real tight. You can say anything you want, right to his face. He's real nice." "Well," said his Aunt Pearl, "I always did say there are some nice white people."

Whether or not there is more to these citations than "Some of my best friends are . . ." or "Yes, but you're different," the wall between us remained, or better, the chain-link fence, since despite the barriers we were able to look at each other, walk alongside each other, talk and occasionally touch fingers. When two people stand up close to the fence on either side, without touching it, they can look through the interstices and forget that they are looking through a fence.

The disadvantage of being white was offset in part by the fact that, as an outsider, I was not a competitor. Thus, in the matter of skin color, I saw myself nowhere in the spectrum of black- to light-skinned (or "bright"); I was completely out of it, with no vested interest. It could be that this made it possible for some people to speak freely to me about skin color.

> "You know, I'm the darkest one in my family. All my aunts, uncles, everybody is light-skinned and they were all down on me, except my grandmother. . . . She'd do anything for me, maybe because she saw everyone else against me. . . . All the time I was coming up, I kept hoping somebody would have a baby darker than me."

Looking at me, however, the people I came to know in the area probably saw more than a "white male adult." They saw or knew many other things as well, any one of which relegated me to outside status. Those with whom I was in regular contact knew, for example, that I was with them because it was my job to be with them, and they knew, according to their individual comprehension and my ability to communicate, just what my job was. They knew that I lived outside the area. They knew that I was a college graduate, or at least they associated an advanced education with the work I was doing. Moreover, it was apparent, certainly to me, that I was not fluent in their language. Thus, I was an outsider not only because of race, but also because of occupation, education, residence, and speech. The fact that I was Jewish came up only twice. Once, a man who worked but did not live in the area threw some Yiddish expressions at me because "I thought you looked Jewish." The other time was when I met a soldier in a local bootleg joint. We had been talking for some ten minutes or so when he asked me whether I was "Eyetalian." I told him I was Jewish. "That's just as good," he said. "I'm glad you're not white."

The fact that I was married and a father, and that I was bigger than average size—6′1″, 185 pounds—probably didn't matter much, except as they entered incidentally into my personal relationship with one or another individual. Since the people I spent most of my time with ranged in age from twenty to the middle forties, I would guess that my age (thirty-seven) was not significant in itself.

On several different counts I was an outsider[2] but I also was a participant in a full sense of the word. The people I was observing knew that I was observing them, yet they allowed me to participate in their activities and take part in their lives to a degree that continues to surprise me. Some "exploited" me, not as an outsider but rather as one who, as a rule, had more resources than they did. When one of them came up with the resources—money or a car, for example—he too was "exploited" in the same way. I usually tried to limit money or other favors to what I thought each would

---

2. From the outset, I had decided that I would never shoot crap, pool, or play cards for money, or bet money in any way (numbers excepted, since playing numbers is safely impersonal), and would meticulously avoid the slightest suspicion of a personal involvement with any woman. These self-imposed restrictions to some extent did underline my marginality. My explanation that I couldn't afford to chance a fight or bad feelings because of my job was usually accepted and I was generally excused from participating in these activities rather than excluded from them.

have gotten from another friend had he the same resources as I. I tried to meet requests as best I could without becoming conspicuous. I was not always on the giving end and learned somewhat too slowly to accept food or let myself be treated to drinks even though I knew this would work a hardship on the giver.

When in the field, I participated as fully and as whole-mindedly as I could, limited only by my own sense of personal and professional propriety and by what I assumed to be the boundaries of acceptable behavior as seen by those I was with.

Occasionally, when I wanted to record a physical description of say, a neighborhood, an apartment, or a social event, I tried to be an observer only. In practice, I found it impossible to keep all traces of participation out of a straight observer role.

One Saturday night, with my observer role clearly in mind, I went to a dance at the Capitol Arena where more than a thousand people were jammed together. I was the only white male, this was my first time at such an event, the music was so foreign to me that I picked out the wrong beat, and I was unable to identify several of the band instruments. I was, willy-nilly, an observer. But here are a few lines excerpted from the field observation:

> It was very hot, it was very noisy, it was very smelly, and it was all very exciting. It was impossible to remain simply an observer in a place like this, even for someone as phlegmatic as I. It was only a few minutes after Jackie Wilson started singing that I discovered that the noise wasn't nearly loud enough, the heat wasn't nearly hot enough, and the odor from more than a thousand closely packed people was not really strong enough at all. Like everyone else, I wanted more of everything.

Almost from the beginning, I adopted the dress and something of the speech of the people with whom I was in most frequent contact, as best I could without looking silly or feeling uncomfortable. I came close in dress (in warm weather, tee or sport shirt and khakis or other slacks) with almost no effort at all. My vocabulary and diction changed, but not radically. Cursing and using ungrammatical constructions at times—though they came easily—did not make any of my adaptations confusable with the speech of the street. Thus, while remaining conspicuous in speech and perhaps in dress, I had dulled some of the characteristics of my background. I probably made myself more accessible to others, and certainly more acceptable to myself. This last point was forcefully brought home to me one evening when, on my way to a professional meeting, I stopped off at the Carry-out in a suit and tie. My loss of ease made me clearly aware that the change in dress, speech, and general carriage was as important for its effect on me as it was for its effect on others.

In retrospect, it seems as if the degree to which one becomes a participant is as much a matter of perceiving oneself as a participant as it is of being accepted as a participant by others.

REFERENCES

Bazelon, David L. Address to the Federal Bar Association, National Press Club, Washington, D.C., April 30, 1963. (Mimeographed)

Becker, Howard S. "Problems of Inference and Proof in Participant-Observation," *American Sociological Review*, XXIII, No. 6 (Dec. 1958), 652–660.

Bendix, Reinhart, and Seymour M. Lipset, eds. *Class, Status and Power*. Glencoe: The Free Press, 1953.

Blood, Robert O., and Donald M. Wolfe. *Husband and Wives: The Dynamics of Married Living*. Glencoe: The Free Press, 1960.

Bott, Elizabeth. *Family and Social Network*. London: Tavistock Publications, Ltd., 1957.

Burgess, E. W., and D. J. Bogue, eds. *Contributions to Urban Sociology*. Chicago: University of Chicago Press, 1946.

Chandler, Margaret. "The Social Organization of Workers in a Rooming House Area." Unpublished Ph.D. dissertation, University of Chicago, 1948.

Cloward, Richard A., and Lloyd E. Ohlin. *Delinquency and Opportunity: A Theory of Delinquent Gangs*. Glencoe: The Free Press, 1960.

Cohen, Albert K. *Delinquent Boys*. Glencoe: The Free Press, 1955.

Cohen, Albert K., and Harold Hodges, Jr. "Characteristics of the Lower-Blue-Collar-Class," *Social Problems*, X, No. 4 (1963), 303–334.

Davis, Allison. "The Motivation of the Underprivileged Worker." Ch. V of William F. Whyte, ed., *Industry and Society.* New York: McGraw-Hill, 1946.

Drake, St. Clair, and Horace Cayton. *Black Metropolis.* New York: Harcourt, Brace, 1945.

Frazier, E. Franklin. *The Negro Family in the United States.* Chicago: University of Chicago Press, 1939.

Gans, Herbert J. *The Urban Villagers.* New York: The Free Press of Glencoe, 1962.

————. "The Negro Family: Reflections on the Moynihan Report," *Commonweal,* LXXXIII, No. 2 (Oct. 15, 1965), 47–51.

Gladwin, Thomas. "The Anthropologist's View of Poverty," in National Conference on Social Welfare, *The Social Welfare Forum,* 1961. New York: Columbia University Press, 1961, pp. 73–86.

Health and Welfare Council of the National Capital Area. *1960 Index of Social and Economic Deprivation of Neighborhoods in the District of Columbia.*

Henry, Jules. "The Personal Community and Its Invariant Properties," *American Anthropologist,* LX, No. 5 (Oct. 1958), 827–831.

Hoebel, E. Adamson. *The Law of Primitive Man: A Study in Comparative Legal Dynamics.* Cambridge: Harvard University Press, 1954.

Hughes, Everett C. *Men and Their Work.* Glencoe: The Free Press, 1958.

Inkeles, Alex. "Industrial Man," *American Journal of Sociology,* LXVI, No. 1 (July, 1960), 1–31.

Kinsey, Alfred C., Wardell B. Pomeroy, and Clyde E. Martin. "Social Level and Sexual Outlet," in Reinhart Bendix and Seymour M. Lipset, eds. *Class, Status and Power.* Glencoe: The Free Press, 1953, pp. 300–308.

Klein, Josephine. *Samples from English Cultures.* 2 vols. London: Routledge and Kegan Paul, 1965.

Lewis, Hylan. "Culture, Class and the Behavior of Low Income Families." Paper prepared for Conference on Views of Lower Class Culture, New York City, June 27–29, 1963. (Mimeographed)

————. "Discussion of [Marian R. Yarrow's] 'Problems of Methods in Family Studies.'" Paper presented at the National Conference on Social Welfare, New York City, May 29, 1962. (Mimeographed)

Lewis, Oscar. *The Children of Sanchez: Autobiography of a Mexican Family.* New York: Random House, 1961.

————. "Further Observations on the Folk-Urban Continuum and Urbanization with Special Reference to Mexico City." N.d. (Mimeographed)

Merton, Robert K. *Social Theory and Social Structure*. Rev. ed. Glencoe: The Free Press, 1957.

Miller, Herman P. *Rich Man, Poor Man*. New York: Crowell, 1964.

Miller, S. M. "The American Lower Classes: A Typological Approach," Jan. 1963. (Mimeographed)

Miller, S. M., and Frank Riessman. "The Working Class Subculture: A New View," *Social Problems*, IX, No. 1 (1961), 86–97.

Miller, Walter B. "Cultural Features of An Urban Lower Class Community." U.S. Public Health Service, 1957. (Mimeographed)

———. "Implications of Urban Lower-Class Culture for Social Work," *Social Service Review*, XXXIII, No. 3, (Sept. 1959), pp. 219–236.

———. "Lower Class Culture as a Generating Milieu of Deliquency," *Journal of Social Issues*, XIV, No. 3, (1958), pp. 5–19.

———. Foreword to Sydney E. Bernard, *Fatherless Families: Their Economic and Social Adjustment*. Brandeis University Papers in Social Welfare, No. 7. 1964.

Myrdal, Gunnar, with Richard Sterner and Arnold Rose. *An American Dilemma*. New York: Harper, 1944.

Nadel, S. F. *The Theory of Social Structure*. Glencoe: The Free Press, 1957.

Orshansky, Mollie. "Counting the Poor: Another Look at the Poverty Profile," *Social Security Bulletin* (Social Security Administration, U.S. Department of Health, Education and Welfare), (Jan. 1965), pp. 3–29.

Rainwater, Lee. "Work and Identity in the Lower Class." Paper prepared for Washington University Conference on Planning for the Quality of Urban Life, April, 1965. (Mimeographed)

———. "Work and Identity in the Lower Class," in Sam Bass Warner, Jr., *Planning for a Nation of Cities*. Cambridge: Forthcoming.

Reiff, Robert, and Frank Riessman. "The Indigenous Nonprofessional: A Strategy of Change in Community Action and Community Mental Health Programs." National Institute of Labor Education Mental Health Program, Report Number 3, Nov. 1964. (Mimeographed)

Robb, J. H. *Working-Class Anti-Semite*. London: Tavistock, 1954.

Rodman, Hyman. "The Lower-Class Value Stretch," *Social Forces*, XLII, No. 2 (Dec. 1963), 205–215.

Rohrer, John and Munro Edmonson. *The Eighth Generation: Cultures and Personalities of New Orleans Negroes*. New York: Harper and Row, 1960.

Rosenberg, Morris. *Society and the Adolescent Self-Image*. Princeton: Princeton University Press, 1965.

Sherif, Muzafer and Carolyn. "Youth in Their Groups in Different Settings." Paper prepared for the Conference on Views of Lower Class Culture, New York City, June 27–29, 1963. (Mimeographed)

Slobodin, Richard. " 'Upton Square': A Field Report and Commentary." Child Rearing Study, Health and Welfare Council of the National Capital Area, 1960. (Mimeographed)

U.S. Bureau of the Census. *Methodology and Scores of Socioeconomic Status*, Working Paper No. 15, Washington, D.C., 1963.

U.S. Department of Labor, Office of Policy Planning and Research. *The Negro Family: The Case for National Action* (The Moynihan Report). March, 1965.

Whyte, William Foote. *Street Corner Society*. 2nd ed., Chicago: University of Chicago Press, 1955.

———. "On Street Corner Society," in E. W. Burgess and D. J. Bogue, eds., *Contributions to Urban Sociology*. Chicago: University of Chicago Press, 1964, pp. 256–268.

———. "A Slum Sex Code," in Reinhart Bendix and Seymour Lipset, eds., *Class, Status and Power*. Glencoe: The Free Press, 1953, pp. 308–316.

———, ed. *Industry and Society*. New York: McGraw-Hill, 1946.

INDEX

ABOUT THE AUTHOR

Elliot Liebow (1925–1994) served as chief of the Center for the Study of Work and Mental Health of the National Institute of Mental Health. Liebow wrote *Tally's Corner* as his Ph.D. dissertation at the Catholic University of America. He also published *Tell Them Who I Am*, a study of homeless women in America, in 1993.